The Grail

The
Grail
A Secret History

JOHN MATTHEWS

BARRON'S

To David Franzoni for his friendship
and enthusiasm.

First edition for North America published by
Barron's Educational Series, Inc., 2006

First published 2005 under the title THE GRAIL
by Godsfield, a division of Octopus Publishing Group Ltd,
2-4 Heron Quays, London E14 4JP

All inquiries should be addressed to:
Barron's Educational Series, Inc.
250 Wireless Blvd.
Hauppauge, NY 11788
www.barronseduc.com

ISBN-13: 978-0-7641-5867-4
ISBN-10: 0-7641-5867-8

Library of Congress Catalog No. 2004115896

Printed and bound in China
9 8 7 6 5 4 3 2 1

CONTENTS

INTRODUCTION

I have been searching for the Grail for most my life. In fact, it is almost 30 years since I began to explore the myths surrounding this most mysterious of objects. During this time I have pursued many different theories; indeed, new ones seem to crop up every year. Yet to date, I have found none that is satisfying. Most seem concerned to discover the whereabouts of a physical object, to trace some mysterious origin or, more recently, to discover within the stories of the Grail hidden patterns of history, lost windows onto the past.

Most of the theories contain something of interest, most are entertaining, and some are genuinely inspiring. Yet it seems to me that in seeking this kind of answer to the riddle of the Grail, we are looking in the wrong place.

During three decades spent poring over dusty books and manuscripts, I have often felt like one of King Arthur's knights, endlessly following overgrown pathways, delving ever more deeply into the great forest of Arthurian tradition. In all that time I have never once come across anything to indicate that the Grail itself ever actually existed in the physical world.

What I have found is the trace of an idea, a strand of belief in the infinite, a story of an endless quest for truth. The Grail is best understood as a *meme*, to borrow a word from the scientific community, the cultural equivalent of a gene, an idea born at the beginning of human history, embedded so deeply within our consciousness that we are scarcely aware of it, though it remains very much alive in us today.

This Grail is not a physical object, but rather an idea carried by history and by some of our greatest works of literature. Above all, it is a dream that all may follow, a lifelong journey that winds itself in and around our daily lives like a golden thread.

This book represents the current status of my own search. It should still be seen not as a final statement, but as an interim report. At this moment, I have no idea where the quest will lead me next, into what new avenues of thought, imagery, and symbolism that will be needed to enable me to reach my goal. I have tried to outline something like a narrative history, following the Grail from the earliest references to the present time, when so many new theories and speculations have been advanced that seem to hide the truth about the Grail more deeply rather than to uncover it.

The journey is chronological as far as is possible, though there are gaps and places where the trail doubles back on itself or is lost in the trackless wastes of esoteric spirituality. In essence, there are two chronologies, which often run side by side – the events of history both reflect and are reflected in the literature of the time (for example, the Crusades), while in many cases the authors of the medieval Grail romances look back to the time of the historical Jesus in order to establish links with the Arthurian Grail quest.

There are periods of time when the Grail hid itself so deeply that few even knew of its existence. Yet it was never completely forgotten, and no matter how far in time or space we have to travel between one point and another, the Grail always reappears, sometimes taking on a new form, sometimes echoing an older manifestation, but always retaining certain key elements: the ability to transform, to enlighten, to inspire – to lead its seekers into ever more fascinating places. In each instance where the Grail story has borrowed from other cultures and symbologies, the point at which these encounters first occur will be discussed there, rather than at the historical moment in time where they first appeared.

Some of the images, especially the earliest, may be unfamiliar to followers of the Grail myth, and some readers will doubtless disagree with my interpretation. However, within each of these images and strands of belief and tradition some recognizable shadow of the Grail is seen to exist.

The chalice of St Remegius (d.533) resides in the cathedral of Notre Dame in Reims, France. It is one of a number of medieval vessels said to be the Grail.

Beyond this the mystery of the Grail remains impenetrable as it always has and probably always will, as indeed it should. I can think of no more terrible event than the discovery of an object that could somehow be proved, beyond all doubt, to be *the* Grail. This may seem an odd statement to make after spending so much of my life in search of the truth about this mystical vessel. But the fact is that the Grail remains always just out of reach, teasing us with rumours of its existence or its meaning. To discover it in actuality would be to destroy much of what it represents, which, by its very nature can never be wholly uncovered or understood.

Throughout my studies of this unique subject I have tried to remain faithful to one thing: that the truth represented by the Grail, no matter how many times it is reinterpreted, remains essentially unchanged. Just what that truth may be (at least from my perspective) will be revealed during the course of this book.

THE ESSENTIAL STORY

What we might call the central Grail myth has almost as many forms as there are texts that tell of it. Many do not agree on the names of the characters, the sequence of events, or the places and times in which these took place. For this reason I have outlined the basic story, synthesized from the medieval Arthurian romances that remain the primary source for what we know about the Grail. This will, I hope, form a jumping-off point from which readers can follow the crossings and recrossings of the various texts we shall encounter in our exploration of the Grail's history

The story begins with Joseph of Arimathea, a wealthy merchant said to be Jesus' uncle, into whose care Christ's body is given for burial. According to some accounts, he also obtained the cup used by Christ to celebrate the Last Supper. While the body is being washed and prepared for the tomb, some blood flows from the wounds, which Joseph catches in this same vessel.

After the Resurrection, Joseph is accused of stealing the body and is thrown into prison and deprived of food. Christ appears to him in a blaze of light and entrusts the cup to his care. He then instructs Joseph in the celebration of the Mass and mystery of the Incarnation before vanishing. After this Joseph is miraculously kept alive by a dove that descends to his cell every day and deposits a holy wafer in the cup. He is finally released in 70 CE, and, joined by his sister and her husband, Bron, goes into exile overseas with a small group of followers. A table called the First Table of the Grail is constructed to represent the table of the Last Supper. Twelve may sit there, but a thirteenth seat remains empty, either in token of Christ's place or that of Judas. When one of the company attempts to sit in it, he is swallowed up, and the seat is thereafter called the Perilous Seat.

Joseph next sails to Europe and then to Britain where he establishes the first Christian church in Glastonbury, dedicating it to the Mother of Christ. Here the Grail is housed and serves as a chalice in celebrations of the Mass in which the whole company participates and which becomes known as the Mass of the Grail.

In other versions Joseph goes no further than Europe, and the guardianship of the Grail passes to Bron, who becomes known as the Rich Fisherman after he miraculously feeds the entire company with a single fish. The company settles at a place called Avaron to await the coming of the third Grail-keeper, Alain.

From here the Grail is taken to Muntsalvache (the Mountain of Salvation), where a temple is built to house it, and an order of Grail knights is established to serve and guard the vessel. They sit together at the Second Table of the Grail and partake of a feast provided by the sacred vessel. A form of Grail Mass once again takes place in which the Grail-keeper, now described as a king, serves as priest. Shortly after, he receives a mysterious wound caused by a fiery spear, in the thigh in some versions or more specifically in the generative organs in other versions. Thereafter, the guardian is known as the Maimed or Wounded King and the countryside around the Grail castle becomes barren and is called the Waste Land – a state explicitly connected with the Grail-lord's wound. The spear with which he is struck becomes identified with the lance of Longinus, the Roman centurion who, in biblical tradition, pierced the side of Christ on the Cross. From this time on there are four objects in the castle – the cup

This painting by William Blake shows Joseph of Arimathea teaching the mysteries of the Grail in Britain.

itself, the spear, a sword that is said to break at a crucial moment, and either a shallow dish or a stone. These are the hallows, the four sacred treasures that must be sought and wielded in a mysterious way by those who seek the Grail.

THE ROUND TABLE

By this time we have reached the age of the legendary King Arthur, and the scene is set for the beginning of the great quest. The Round Table, established by the magician Merlin, is known as the Third Table of the Grail (though the vessel itself is absent). In the new king's citadel of Camelot a fellowship of knights, called the Knights of the Round Table, meet and establish a code of chivalry. At Pentecost the Grail makes an appearance, floating on a beam of light through the hall, and each person there receives the food he likes best, whereupon the knights all pledge themselves to seek the holy object.

A medieval illumination showing the youthful Grail knight Galahad, accompanied by a hermit, welcomed at the Round Table.

There follows an extraordinary series of initiatory adventures, featuring five knights in the main: Gawain, Lancelot, Perceval, Galahad, and Bors. Of these and of the many knights who set out from Camelot, only three are destined to achieve the quest. Lancelot, the best knight in the world, fails because of his love for Arthur's queen. Gawain, a splendid figure who may once have been the original Grail knight, is shown in the medieval texts as being too worldly – though he comes close to the heart of the mystery.

For the rest, Galahad, the son of Lancelot and the Grail princess, is destined to sit in the Perilous Seat and to achieve the quest. Perceval, like Gawain originally a successful candidate, is partially ousted by Galahad. While he is permitted to see the Grail and to use the spear to heal the Wounded King, at the end of the quest he returns to the Grail castle, where he apparently becomes its new guardian.

Bors, the last of the three knights to experience the Grail directly, is the humble, dogged, "ordinary" man, who strives with all his being to reach toward the infinite, and succeeds. He voyages with Galahad and Perceval to the holy city of Sarras, far across the Western sea, where the mystery of the Grail is finally achieved. Of the three, Bors alone returns to Camelot to tell what has happened.

One other seeker, Dindrane, Perceval's sister, accompanies the Grail knights on their quest; having given her life for another, she is carried to the city of the Grail and buried in splendor beside Galahad.

Once the Grail is achieved in that time, and since it is fully achieved by only one person, the vessel is withdrawn – but not entirely and not forever. Perceval takes up residence again in the empty castle to await the return of the Grail, which is once again available to all true seekers.

THE EVOLVING STORY

Such is the story in its essentials. It took many hundreds of years for this myth to evolve to the point it has reached today. Many different streams flowed into it, sometimes forcing the central river of the story to overflow its banks – forming new tributaries, some of which dried up and became lost, while others broadened out for a time then shrank again to no more than a trickle. I have tried to follow all of these tributaries as well as the main river of the story itself. Many of these steams flow side by side, connected only by the presence of the Grail; but all flow onward, carrying with them a dream that has been part of our consciousness for as long as history itself has existed. It is these expressions of the Grail mystery, no matter how fleeting, that we shall seek to trace in the pages that follow.

Many friends and colleagues have walked the path of the Grail with me, and I would like to pay tribute to them here – both for the light they have cast on this great mystery and for the companionship they have offered along the way. In particular I would name David Spangler with whom I have spent so many hours discussing the Grail; Gareth Knight and Dolores Ashcroft Nowicki who first opened my eyes to the reality behind the idea; Ari Berk for the many wise and witty insights he has shared with me over the years; Freya Reeves, Karen Ralls, and Marian Green for being my soul-sisters on the quest; Linda Malcor for illuminating conversations about the Sarmatians and the Narts; Mark Ryan for being there and for a wild ride to Royston nearly 20 years ago; Payam Narbarz for invaluable insights into the mysteries of Jamshid; my editor Brenda Rosen for all her wise help and advice over the years; but most of all my wife Caitlín, who had put up with my Grail-seeking habit for almost as long as I have been engaged in it and lent her own wonderfully deep knowledge at a thousand points on the trail. Toward the end of the work on this book, she stepped up to the task and helped me to complete it, for which I owe her more thanks than I can say.

Finally, I would like to thank some very special people – the members of the Lorian Association and Dwina Murphy-Gibb, who together made it possible for me to complete this book during a difficult time. To them I offer my eternal gratitude.

To all of these named and to the legion of Grail-seekers and scholars, known and unknown, wise and foolish, who have kept the idea of the quest alive through the ages, a huge thank you. Many of you will almost certainly disagree with my conclusions, but if they encourage you to seek further, I will be more than happy.

JOHN MATTHEWS
OXFORD, 2005

The Titan's Goblet *(1833) by Thomas Cole shows an imaginative image of the Krater, the vast mixing bowl of the gods.*

ANCIENT SHADOWS

*He considered [the] chalices offered at every alter ... Of all material things still
discoverable in the world the Graal had been nearest the Divine and Universal
Heart. Sky and sea and land were moving, not towards the vessel but to all it
symbolized and had held ... and through that gate ... all creation moved.*[129]

CHARLES WILLIAMS *WAR IN HEAVEN*

Just how old is the Grail? The answer may come as a surprise to some: that it is a
great deal older than the Christian era and its terrain is more extensive than the period
when the Arthurian myths made it familiar throughout the Western world. In fact, the
oldest references come not from the Celtic or medieval Christian sources with which
we are most familiar, but from a far earlier time. In both classical Greek myths and
the Vedic hymns of ancient India, dating from many hundreds of years before the
beginning of Christianity, there are references that point directly to the Grail, while in
the Persian Empire, an object displaying many of the qualities of the Grail also
flourished. Even earlier, in the prehistoric world of our distant ancestors, it is possible
to see a type of proto-Grail in the very first objects crafted by human hands.

But tracing such ancient, preliterate references can be done only if there is an
established frame of reference from which to work. In the case of the Grail, this means
looking at the ideas underlying the medieval texts that describe it in such detail. The
story already exists in its essential form. From here it is possible to work backwards
to locate other sacred objects that share the qualities and bring about the same effects
as the later Grail stories.

The first point to recognize is that in all of the later texts the Grail is perceived not
just as a sacred object, but as something that comes directly from a divine source and
serves as a medium by which human beings can draw close to the deity. This is the
prime motivation in the medieval stories of the Grail quest, in which the knights who
go forth in search of the marvelous vessel do so not only because it is a great
adventure, but because they want to draw closer to God.

The second factor, present in virtually every reference to the Grail in both early
and late pagan and Christian sources, is that what the vessel *contains* is often more

important than the vessel itself. Thus, at the conclusion of the great medieval quests, when the Grail knight drinks from the holy chalice or looks into it, he discovers something within that connects him directly with a spiritual source. There are a number of scenes where the quest knights receive such visions of the Grail. One such is found in Sir Thomas Malory's fifteenth-century masterpiece *Le Morte D'Arthur*, which gathered up the scattered fragments of Arthurian and Grail literature and molded them into the first true English novel. It comes from close to the end of the book when the great quest is almost over and describes the final mystical transformation of the pure knight, Sir Galahad.

Now [Galahad] rose up early [as did] his fellows, and came to the palace, and [they] saw before them the Holy Vessel, and a man kneeling on his knees in likeness of a Bishop, that had about him a great fellowship of angels … and … he arose and began a mass of Our Lady. And when he came to the sacrament of the Mass, and had done, he called Galahad, and said to him: 'Come forth the servant of Jesu Christ, and thou shall see that which thou hast much desired to see.' And then Galahad [looked within the Grail and] began to tremble right hard when the deadly flesh began to behold the spiritual things. Then he held up his hands toward heaven and said: 'Lord, I thank thee, for now I see that which has been my desire many a day. Now, Blessed Lord, would I no longer live, if it might please thee Lord.' And there the Bishop took Our Lord's body betwixt his hands, and proffered it to Galahad, and he received it right gladly and meekly. 'Now what thou who I am?' said the good man. 'Nay,' said Galahad. 'I am Joseph, son of Joseph of Arimathea, whom Our Lord hath sent here to bear thee fellowship …'

Galahad, Perceval, and Bors kneel in awe before the Grail, in this illumination from the Queste del Saint Graal (c.1470).

> *And when he had said these words, Galahad went to Perceval and kissed him, and commended him to God, and so he went to Sir Bors and kissed him, and commended him to God, and said: 'Sir, salute me to my lord, Sir Lancelot, my father, and as soon as you see him, remind him of this unstable world.' And therewith he kneeled down before the table and made his prayers, and then suddenly his soul departed to Jesu Christ, and a great multitude of angels bare his soul up to heaven, that the two fellows might well behold it.*[79]

Galahad's innocence and his desire to encounter God directly mean that he cannot live in the human world any longer. Like many of the saints of medieval literature he passes from this world with none of the struggle that normally accompanies death.

The third aspect of the Grail in these stories is that it transforms those who come into its presence. Just as Galahad is transformed by looking into the holy cup, so virtually all the references in the earliest literature refer to vessels that give food, inspiration, even life itself to those who eat or drink from them, and that those who do so are changed forever. When looking backwards across the ages to find the oldest original points of reference for the Grail, we are therefore seeking objects that possess all of these qualities: the connection with a spiritual source, the ability to transform those who approach it, and the containing of a mysterious substance.

THE GRAIL OF PREHISTORY

It is not necessary to look very far among the archaeological remains and documents from the ancient world to find such objects. The history and *modus operandi* of these vessels not only look forward to the more familiar Grail of the medieval era; they offer vital clues to understanding the true nature of the Grail itself.

The oldest vessels of divine origin and substance derive from a period when the great foundation myths of the world were first established, when our earliest ancestors began to perceive everything around them as having a divine source. Pre-literate cultures, possessing no writing, preserved their first insights into the cosmos orally or through the creation of physical objects. By the time these ideas were finally written down, they had become fixed and codified, accepted truths seen as issuing from the mouths of the gods themselves. They were thus already immeasurably old when they were first recorded in written form.

The fact that the idea of the divine vessel is found in the very first records of human history shows that our earliest ancestors recognized the importance of such objects, and they held great significance for them. It is possible to imagine how the earliest cave dwellers, speculating on their own origins, came to see a vessel like the ones from which they ate and drank every day as a distant echo of the divine vessels in which the gods had mixed the very elements that gave them life.

It cannot be known how the first artificers understood their own creations, but the natural beauty and grace with which the oldest man-made vessels are imbued suggest that these were not just made to be containers, but also objects of beauty that reflected a divine prototype. Imagine one of the first artisans of the preliterate world creating a vessel that would be used every day to contain life-preserving water or food. It would have been easy to make a rough container without any beauty or gracefulness, but a natural mystical awareness imposed itself on the maker, so that what emerged was an object of beauty, which transcended its utilitarian purpose.

It is possible to see in these first objects crafted by human hands a direct link to the great chalices of later ages created from precious metals and decorated with gems but intended, like the first vessels, to reflect the perfection of a divine creation.

This elegantly crafted beaker from Winterslow in Wiltshire, England, shows how everyday vessels transcended the ordinary in prehistoric life.

THE VESSEL OF THE GODS

In the light of such beliefs it is scarcely surprising that several cultures of the ancient world held the idea that the elements of creation were mixed by the gods in a great vessel before being poured forth to form the cosmos. In the earliest records of the classical world, dating back as far as 2000 BCE, there are references to one such vessel, called the Krater – a mixing bowl from which the gods poured forth the constellations, and drops of matter fell and solidified into the planets of our own familiar solar system. The Greek philosopher Plato (*c*.427–348 BCE), who recorded many of the oldest myths in his works, described the Krater as follows:

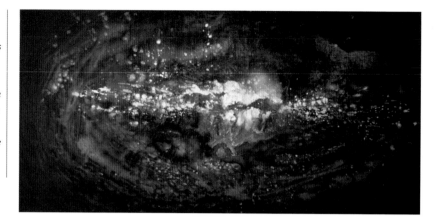

According to Classical Greek tradition, the gods poured forth the galaxy from a huge vessel known as the Krater. This image of a galaxy in cloud shows the appropriateness of the idea.

Thus he [the Creator] spoke, and once more into the cup in which he had previously mingled the soul of the universe he poured the remains of the elements, and mingled them in much the same manner; they were not, however, pure as before, but diluted to the second and third degree. And having made it he divided the whole mixture into souls equal in number to the stars and assigned each soul to a star ... and [they] would hereafter be called Man.[105]

The primal creator, the god before the gods, who has already formed the mighty pantheon of Greek tradition, is now mixing the elements from which humanity itself will emerge – body and soul, intellect and emotions – the fundamental aspects of our nature mixed in the Krater. No wonder the Grail continues to hold such power for us if it truly derived from such a mighty vessel, for this is literally the womb from which we issued, the divine alembic in which we were first formed, first imbued with the elements that make us unique.

THE DRINK OF IMMORTALITY

If the divine elements of creation were indeed mixed in the Grail or a prototype, then how potent must be the drink distilled within this divine vessel and how powerful and transformative that drink must be when imbibed by humans! It is clear to see how later Christian writers and compilers of the Grail texts drew parallels between these ancient ideas and traditions and those of their own nascent God. Three cultures – one of which contains the beginning of the Grail myth proper and the other two, which may have influenced it – describe such a sacred drink as well as the vessel that contained it. Despite being separated by time and distance, more than one commentator has pointed out parallels between the cultures of ancient India and Celtic Europe. It seems more than accidental that both tell of sacred vessels and of a divine drink, which, when partaken of by humans, could effect such a powerful transformation.

The ephedra plant is believed to be the source of the divine drink of Vedic India known as soma.

It is in the Vedic traditions of ancient India, which may date back to 2000 BCE, that many of these ideas first appear, especially in the teachings relating to the divine drink known as soma. According to the oldest of these traditions, soma originated on a sacred mountain, Mujavat. Soma is also known as "the milk of heaven," which places it outside the human world and aligns it with the pouring forth of creation from the Krater. As with many such life-giving substances, such as fire stolen by Prometheus in the Greek traditions, the god Agni stole soma from the Castle of Brass, where it was guarded by a group of angelic beings known as the Gandharvas. He escaped in the form of an eagle, then gave it to man, who used it as a means of connecting with the source of all being.

But soma is not always seen as a drink; it is sometimes referred to as a living being who must be sacrificed and consumed. It is also described as a "king" who lives in a castle from which he must be symbolically released. Parallels between the Christian Eucharist and the Zoroastrian *haoma* rites are strong here, and we may also see King Soma as having influenced the figure of the wounded Grail king of the later medieval romances who can be released from eternal torment only when the mysteries of the Grail are achieved.

There are many contenders for the possible identity of the plant from which soma is derived; the most likely seems to be a small shrub *Ephedra intermedia*, which when crushed gives forth either a golden or milky substance. When drunk, this produces a mild euphoria said to be "more than the comfort of strength but less than intoxication," which enables the drinker to attain oneness with God – surely the objective of all Grail-seekers.

The method of harvesting and preparing soma echoes that of the mistletoe plant gathered by the Druids in Britain. In both instances the plant is cut with a sacred knife and laid upon an unbleached cloth. Mistletoe, which is a much more hallucinogenic (and poisonous) substance than *Ephedra intermedia*, also produces a milky substance; both it and soma have been referred to as the semen of the gods and are said to represent a sacrificial element in the rites of both cultures.

Soma is also believed to contain many of the elements of creation, so that to partake of it is to partake of the substance of life itself, as well as of the gods. Poets and mystics value it as a divine drink of inspiration, while others declare that it is part of a holy exchange between mortals and gods whereby humans aspire to godhead and the gods lean toward mortality.

Despite the fact that soma is described in such a bewildering array of symbolic terms, underlying all of these is an essential pattern, which is repeated in the later Grail myth. Soma is a life-giving drink that allows communion with deity. Where it is more specifically described in terms of a king who rules over a castle (like the castle of the Grail, often situated on top of a mountain) there are clear echoes of the later Grail story. A glance at one of the hymns from the *Rig Veda* will provide evidence:

> *I have tasted, as one who knows it secret,*
> *the honeyed drink that charms and relaxes,*
> *the drink that all, both gods and mortals,*
> *seek to obtain, calling it nectar.*
>
> *We have drunk the soma and become immortal!*
> *We have attained the light, we have found the Gods!*
> *What can the malice of mortal Man*
> *or his spite, O immortal, do to us now?*[104]

The language here could easily come from almost any one of the later Grail texts. Once again we see the divine drink offering a connection between man and god. Since Vedic tradition makes both humanity and the gods equal partners in the adventure of life, it is easy to see how the traditions of soma can be related both to the ideas expressed in Plato's myth of the Krater and to the medieval Grail quest, which in both instances lead to unions with a deity.

Whether these ancient Vedic texts should be seen as having influenced the growth of the Grail myth remains an open question. However, there is evidence pointing to contact between the cultures of ancient India and of the European Celts, which share a number of beliefs, including the idea of reincarnation, the afterlife, and the participation of the gods in human

This bronze cauldron, found at Gundestrup in Denmark, embodies the Celtic belief in a divine vessel.

affairs. One of the most famous cult objects of the Celtic world, the Gundestrup Cauldron, depicts elephants among the animals inscribed upon it. The vessel was discovered in a Danish bog in 1891 and is believed to be of Celtic or La Tène origin dating after 120 BCE. The elephants have led some authorities to speculate that captive artisans from the Indian subcontinent may have worked on its design. Certainly there are sufficient parallels between some of the teachings contained in the Vedas and those found in the literature of the Celts to suggest that influence may have flowed between the two cultures at an early date.

THE CUP OF JAMSHID

Further east, in the vast Persian Empire, flourished another vessel that displays many elements that would later find a home in the Grail myth. This was the Cup of Jamshid. According to the eleventh-century historian Firdausi, Jamshid, a semidivine king said to have ruled over the ancient world, was the grandson of Prince Kumars, the Persian Adam, and was the fifth king to rule after the creation of the world. He is credited with a thousand-year reign, during which time he instituted the mysteries of warfare, spinning, and agriculture. At the end of his long life he sought to be worshipped as a god and therefore had his power taken away by the creator.[31] His magical cup enabled him to discover whatever was taking place in the world. Once again this suggests an ancient memory of a vessel that had perhaps contained all the elements of creation.

The Persian semi-divine King Jamshid, shown in this thirteenth-century miniature, possessed a cup that could bring enlightenment to those who drank from it.

The Cup of Jamshid also represented kingship, perhaps in its divine form, passed down through the ages in the royal line of the Persian and Iranian empires. This could be seen as a precursor to the long line of Grail kings who guarded the sacred vessel. It could also be said that the cup offered a connection with the divine origins of the world, just as do all the sacred vessels at which we have been looking.

THE SAMPO

The Greeks and the people of ancient India and Persia were not the only cultures to know of such extraordinary sacred vessels. On the vast open plains of the steppes nomadic tribespeople told stories of a cauldron that possessed otherworldly qualities, while in the Finno-Ugric traditions of northern Europe a great vessel, the Sampo, is described as having contained the universe within it.

The creation of the Sampo is described in a vast collection of Finnish legends known as the *Kalevala*, which contains material dating back several thousand years before it was collected and compiled in the nineteenth century. Here the great smith god Ilmarinen is asked to create the Sampo by his brother Vainamoinen, the oldest of the gods. Ilmarinen took feathers from a swan, milk from a barren heifer, a small amount of barley grain, and the finest sheep's wool and placed these in his furnace. He then summoned slaves to stoke the fire until it roared and belched forth flames. Each day Ilmarinen examined the contents of the forge to see what had been created there.

Many marvelous objects came from within the furnace, among them a golden bowl, a red copper ship, a golden-horned heifer, and a plough with silver-tipped handles, golden blade, and copper frame. Yet none of these satisfied Ilmarinen, and each one was broken and thrown back into the inferno. The tenth-century rune of the *Kalevala*, as translated by W. F. Kirby, describes what happened next:

The Finnish smith god Ilmarinen forges the divine vessel of the Sampo, which may be seen as a forerunner of the Grail.

Then the wind arose in fury,
Blew the east wind, blew the west wind,
And the south wind yet more strongly,
And the north wind howled and
  blustered.
Thus they blew one day, a second,
And upon the third day likewise.
Fire was flashing from the windows,
From the door the sparks were flying
And the dust arose to heaven;
With the clouds the smoke was mingled,
Then again smith Ilmarinen,
On the evening of the third day,
Stooped him down, and gazed intently
To the bottom of the furnace,
And he saw the Sampo forming,
With its many-coloured cover.
Thereupon smith Ilmarinen,
He the great primeval craftsmen,
Welded it and hammered at it,
Heaped his rapid blows upon it,
Forged in cunning art the Sampo.[61]

This marvelous object is sometimes described as a great cauldron inscribed with starry patterns (a fact that makes it likely to have been similar to the Krater). According to the oldest version of the *Kalevala*, on one side of it was a flour mill, on another side a salt mill, and on the third side a coin mill. These features alone make it clear that the Sampo is an object that combines elements that would ensure the life of the people. Even the wonderful objects that Ilmarinen destroyed and that must have been reconstituted in the final form taken by the Sampo are very much part of an ancient creation myth. Ploughshares, cups, and mills are all part of the pattern of agricultural life, while coins are the lifeblood of commerce. All are central to the livelihood of the people. The Sampo itself was so powerful that it was mysteriously able to transform the snowy wasteland of the Pohjola province into a green paradise. Later it was broken into pieces that were sought after by various heroes in a manner that once again reflects the quest for the Grail.

THE NARTAMONGA

Further east, on the vast plains of the steppes, a group of nomadic tribespeople known as the Sarmatians, who originated in an area roughly between the Black Sea and the Caspian Sea, preserved another myth of a sacred vessel.

The Sarmatians, shown here in a detail from Trajan's column, told stories of a sacred vessel very like the Grail.

After an encounter with the Roman Emperor Marcus Aurelius in the second century CE, 5500 of these remarkable warriors were assigned to the distant province of Britain as part of the occupying force. Their commander was a Roman officer named Lucius Artorius Castus, who, it has been suggested, was the inspiration for the medieval King Arthur. The stories and deeds of the Sarmatian warriors might have influenced the creation of the chivalric adventures of Arthur's knights. Apart from a considerable amount of historical and archaeological evidence that supports this theory, a number of stories and myths originating with these people are reflected in key elements of the Grail story.

One particular tribe, who are known today as the Narts and who are descendants of the original Sarmatians, have preserved a number of ancient myths, several of which have parallel themes to the Arthurian cycle. One such is the story relating to the Nartamonga, a cauldron-like vessel that would only cook food for heroes and triggered

inspiration in the warriors who possessed it. A story that centers on the hero Batradz, whose deeds strongly echo those of Arthur, can be summarized as follows.

The Narts were quarrelling among themselves over who should keep the Nartamonga, the sacred cup that would serve only the most perfect hero and for which they had sought for a long time in a manner similar to that of the Arthurian knights after the Grail. First Urzymag said that without him they would not have succeeded in their quest for the cup, so he should have it. Then Soslan and Sozyrykn each claimed to be the greatest hero. In each case Batradz, who was the leader of the Narts, refuted their claims, instancing times when they had failed to live up to the highest standards of heroism. Finally, Batradz challenged any man there to find one time when he had failed them. No one could do so, and he therefore got to keep the Nartamonga.

This fifth-century BCE *Scythian gold cup* may *well be an echo of the sacred vessel possessed by the tribe known as the Narts.*

Interestingly, not only is Batradz a prototype of the later King Arthur, he is also a guardian of the Grail, as Arthur himself becomes in the medieval versions of the tale. The nature of the Nartamonga and its ability to enhance heroic abilities and bring inspiration to the one who owns it highlight its similarity with Celtic cauldrons of inspiration and life, which will be examined in the next chapter. There is little room for doubt that the Nart sagas represent an important link in the chain of the Grail's chronology.

So many themes and ideas found within the later history of the Grail were first discovered within these early references that it is difficult not to see a direct line of transmission flowing from the prehistoric religious beliefs of our ancestors, through the increasingly sophisticated theology of the ancient world, into the northern steppes where the Narts carried their sacred cauldron of inspiration and heroic ideals, to the foundation myths of the Finns. From there it flowed into the visionary writings of the Celts and directly into the great melting pot of Western mysticism and Christian theology that produced the first stories featuring the Grail in a form we would recognize today. The Celtic myths provide the all-important bridge connecting the earliest references to the divine vessel to its more familiar appearance in the Christianized mythology of the Arthurian world.

THE CAULDRON
AND ITS KEEPERS

Is it lost, the lonely sea-road of pine and cypress and laurel
That leads to the Sacred Castle over the spun sea-spray?
To the hushed white hall still strewn with its ivory roses and coral
Does the masque of the Lance and the Cup take its marvellous mournful way?

RACHEL ANNAND TAYLOR *PERCEVAL AT CORBENIC*

The idea of a vessel or vessels that offered a direct link to the source of all things or in which the very stuff of creation was contained occurs throughout the oldest records of human history and is central to the history of the Grail. At first this divine vessel is a possession of the gods, something so vast that the whole of creation could fit within it. But as the myth developed, something extraordinary occurred – the vessel was brought directly into the human world. It resided among humans and it could be sought. In some ways this is the most important development in the early history of the Grail – yet it took place largely offstage.

As the first human artificers sought to recreate the idea of the sacred vessel of creation in their everyday cups and beakers, they anchored it in the world forever, making it part of a communal sharing of food and drink. Among the nomadic people of the steppes it became a miraculously everyday object, a cauldron dispensing sustenance both real and spiritual to those who possessed it. Among the Celtic tribes of northern Europe this idea developed further, as a range of magical vessels began to appear in the literature and traditions, bringing with them the idea of a specific guardian of the sacred vessel.

There was no shining cup, no radiant maiden bearing a holy relic through a medieval hall. Instead there were ancient cauldrons, intricately carved, rims set with pearls "warmed by the breath of nine maidens," according to one text. These cauldrons had the power to grant life, to bring forth spiritual food and to bestow upon their owners rare favors. Initially, they were in the keeping of gods and goddesses and only later kept by humankind. In the emerging stories they were stolen

This fifth-century BCE cauldron echoes the stories of famous magical vessels that are described in the mythology of the Celts.

and recovered and stolen again. Hidden and revealed, they lie at the heart of the Celtic mysteries of the Grail, and they were sought after as talismans of power just as the Grail was in the time of King Arthur. By examining this evidence it is possible to see how the reality of the sacred vessel continued throughout the Dark Ages and into the dawn of Christian mysticism. In the process, the form of the sacred vessel changed, preparing the way for the Grail stories to come.

THE CAULDRON OF CERIDWEN

Of all the god- or goddess-owned cauldrons mentioned within Celtic tradition, one of the earliest and most important is that belonging to Ceridwen, an important Celtic female deity who ruled over harvests, pigs, and divine inspiration. The story comes from a collection called *The Mabinogion*, which contains some of the oldest mythic material of the native British Celts.

Ceridwen had a son, Afagddu, which means "utter darkness" or "black crow," whose appearance was so hideous that no one could bear to look upon him. So Ceridwen decided to brew a distillation of pure wisdom and knowledge that would better equip her offspring to deal with life. She began to gather the ingredients that would go into the brew, and she set her servants, an old blind man called Morda and a boy named Gwion, to maintain her great cauldron, which must be kept boiling for a year and a day.

> *As the brew neared completion, Ceridwen went out in search of a few final ingredients, leaving Gwion to stir the mixture. While she was away the youth began to doze, and three drops flew out of the cauldron and scalded his hand. Automatically, he thrust the burned fingers into his mouth and thereby gained all knowledge – for the three drops were the distillation of Ceridwen's brew.*[53]

At once Gwion became aware that the goddess knew what had occurred and that she would come to punish him. With his newfound powers he changed his shape to that of a hare and fled. Ceridwen changed her shape to that of a greyhound and gave chase. Through several more metamorphoses of animal, bird, and fish Gwion fled and the goddess pursued, until finally in desperation he became a grain of wheat in a heap of chaff within a barn. But Ceridwen took the form of a red-crested hen and swallowed the grain. Nine months later she gave birth to a son.

Ceridwen would have killed the child at birth, but he was so beautiful that she put him into a leather bag, which she cast into the sea. The bag floated for nine nights and nine days, or nine moons, until it caught in the salmon weir of the chieftain Gwyddno Garanhir. There it was found by Gwyddno's son, Elffin, an unlucky youth who had lost all his goods and had been awarded the May eve catch of salmon that always came to his father's nets on that day. This time, however, there was no salmon, only a leather bag that squirmed and cried. Bemoaning his evil luck, Elffin took it forth and opened it. Finding the child within, he remarked at once on its beauty, especially its broad white brow. "Taliesin shall I be called," said the child, for the name means "radiant brow," and thus he was called ever after. And though he was still but a newborn child, he made a song for Elffin that was to be the first of many.

Thus, Gwion was reborn from the goddess Ceridwin as Taliesin, who became the greatest bard of the age and went on to prove himself a powerful shaman and prophet in the tradition of Merlin, whose successor he became. All his power came from the cauldron of Ceridwen and the three drops of inspiration that he had accidentally imbibed.

This is an ancient tale and an even older theme. Within it is hidden an initiatory experience in which the candidate was given a drink to send him into a visionary trance where he was able to see both past and future events and was put in touch with divine inspiration. The nature of Gwion's transformations into bird, beast, and fish indicate the shamanic nature of the experience, since all shamans are taught to discover and identify with various totem animals, which become their guides and helpers in the inner realms where they travel to learn the secrets of creation. Taliesin's story is one of the clearest we possess of this initiatory sequence in Celtic tradition. It shows how powerful the experience of the cauldron could be and how it offered a deep and personal connection with the divine at the heart of the universe.

THE CAULDRON OF BRAN

The second example of the Celtic fascination with the divine vessel as cauldron – and one that comes firmly into the realm of the Grail – is that of the demi-god Bran. The story comes once again from the collection of Celtic wonder-tales gathered under the title *The Mabinogion*, which means literally "tales of youth" or perhaps "tales of young heroes."

The Cauldron of Bran *by Alan Lee depicts the giant's head, still telling stories after it had been separated from his shoulders.*

Though not collected until the thirteenth and fourteenth centuries, this work contains most of the oldest Celtic reference to Arthur and the Grail. Within one of these enigmatic tales, "The Story of Branwen, Daughter of Llyr," we find the following account.

Bran the Blessed was king of Britain in the distant past. He arranged for his sister Branwen to marry Matholwch, the king of Ireland. At the wedding feast, Bran's stepbrother, Evnissien, took slight at the Irish king and mutilated his horses. Strife seemed imminent, but Bran offered Matholwch the Cauldron of Rebirth into which dead warriors were placed and came forth alive again. Matholwch already knew of the cauldron, which was originally from Ireland where it was owned by the giant Llassar Llaes Gyfnewid. The giant's wife, Cymedeu Cymeinfoll, gave birth to a fully armed warrior every six weeks. They had been driven out of Ireland and had taken refuge with Bran.

Branwen now went to Ireland where she bore Matholwch a son, but she was so unpopular with the people that she was forbidden her husband's bed and put to work in the kitchens. In sorrow she trained a starling to carry a message to her brother, who came across the sea with all his warriors when he heard of her ill treatment. Matholwch retreated and sued for peace, which was granted on condition that he abdicate in favor of Gwern, his son by Branwen.

At the feast that ensued, Evnissien once again brought disaster by thrusting the child into the fire, where it was consumed. Fighting broke out, and the Irish were winning because they put their fallen warriors into the cauldron, from which they emerged alive. Evnissien, finally remorseful for his misdeeds, crawled inside and, stretching out, broke both the vessel and his own heart. Bran was wounded by a poisoned spear and instructed his seven surviving followers to cut off his head and bear it with them to a specified place.

They journeyed to an island called Gwales, where they were entertained by the head of Bran, which continued to speak and tell tales, and by the singing of the magical birds of Rhiannon, which put them into a trance-like state for 85 years; during this time they knew no fears or hardship and forgot all they had suffered. Then one of the followers opened a door through which they had been forbidden to look or pass, and at once the enchantment ceased and they remembered everything that had happened. Bran's head told them to carry it to London and bury it beneath the White Mount with its face toward France. The seven then returned to Bran's country and found it under the power of a magician named Caswallen. The remainder of the story is told in the next tale in the *The Mabinogion*, but does not concern us here.

Here the cauldron is shown to have definite otherworldly status. The gigantic man and woman, Llassar Llaes Gyfnewid and Cymideu Cymeinfoll, can persuasively be identified with Ceridwen, who was also of gigantic stature, and with Tegid Foel with whom she is partnered in later traditions. Both are said to come from a lake with an island in its center and both possess a wonder-working cauldron. Both couples seem to represent an earlier, more primeval tradition, connected with a race of aboriginal British giants, hinted at elsewhere in Celtic mythology. It is worth remembering that Cymideu was said also to give birth to fully armed warriors every six weeks – perhaps an echo of the way in which the cauldron brings dead warriors back to life. This is surely a clear reference to the sacred vessel as a womb in which elements are combined to bring forth life.

In the story, Matholwch soon discovered the mistake he had made by allowing the couple to remain in his court. They multiplied so rapidly and committed such outrages that in less than four months the Irish king sought to be rid of them. He did this by building a huge iron house for the giants, which was heated in an attempt to destroy his unwanted guests.

In the Irish story the giant and his wife were placed into a vast cauldron-like house of iron in an attempt to destroy them. This is curiously reminiscent of alchemical symbolism, which we shall examine in more detail later, where the alchemical "king" and "queen" are placed in a bath, which is then heated and from which they emerge renewed and transformed. The idea is ultimately the same – those placed into the Cauldron of Rebirth come forth restored.

In "Branwen" the giants escaped to Britain, where they became peaceable citizens. There, unlike the treatment they received in Ireland, they were made welcome and Bran "quartered them throughout every part of the kingdom" – a reference no doubt to the breeding properties of the giantess, whose offspring provide excellent soldiers for the British army!

These elegant Celtic spearheads may have inspired the story of Bran being pierced in the thigh, a theme that reappears in many of the Grail stories.

THE PIERCED THIGH

In this story Bran received a wound from a poisoned spear. He seized Branwen and cried aloud words that are usually translated as "Dogs of Gwern, beware the wrath of Morddwyd Tyllion." This is a very important clue to the connection between the Celtic cauldron myths and the later Grail stories because although Bran's words seem meaningless in the context of the story, when they are translated fully, all becomes clear. "Morddwyd Tyllion" actually means "pierced thigh," and this is a title that is better applied to another character from the Grail story, one not unconnected with Bran. "Dogs of Gwern" have been taken to refer to the Irish followers of the boy Gwern, who is briefly their king. But if the word "gwern" is translated literally, as "alder swamp," the whole sentence then reads "Dogs of the alder swamp [i.e., the Irish] beware the pierced thigh [i.e., Bran]."

The importance of this epithet, as applied to Bran, becomes apparent in looking ahead to the medieval Grail stories. The figure known as the Wounded King suffered a wound in the thigh (generally recognized as referring to the genitals), that could be remedied only by the coming of the destined Grail knight. Remembering that one of the foremost kings of the Grail lineage was named Bron, it is possible to see the links that exist between the titanic figure of Bran and the mystery of the Grail.

Mortally wounded, Bran ordered his surviving followers to cut off his head and take it to Bryn Gwyn, the White Mount in London, and bury it facing toward France. As long as it remained there, he told them, no enemy would be able to invade Britain from that direction. This showed that Bran was recognized as an ancient guardian of the land, a sacred king who continued to watch over the realm after his death.

However, the survivors of the Irish foray did not take a direct route to London. They made two stops along the way – first at Harlech, where Branwen dies, and then at a mysterious island called Gwales, where 80 years passed in feasting and song. During that time, Bran's head continued to speak and entertain the company as though he was still alive; consequently the period is known as the Entertainment of the Noble Head and the seven survivors as the Company of the Noble Head.

THE OTHERWORLDLY FORTRESS

All this evidence points to the island of Gwales as a representation of the Celtic otherworld, where fallen heroes spent a timeless period in feasting and song in the company of their gods. Such a place is clearly a precursor to the paradisal realm later sought by the Grail-seekers. It is also consistent with descriptions of the mysterious island of Caer Siddi, an otherworldly fortress described by Taliesin in a poem called "The Defence of the Chair":

Perfect is my chair in Caer Siddi.
Where no one is afflicted with age or illness …
Three circles of fire surround it,
To its borders come the ocean's currents.
A fruitful fountain plays before it
Whose liquor is sweeter than the finest wine.

Bran was the guardian of the Cauldron of Rebirth; in the "Story of Branwen," after being wounded in the thigh, Bran retired to the otherworld with his followers who were miraculously entertained in the paradisal realm where they felt no sorrow and did not age. Taliesin, who was an initiate and guardian of the mysteries of the cauldron of Ceridwen, described a similar place. Are these the first description we have of the earthly home of the Grail? If so, they are the first of many we will encounter in the search for the truth about the sacred vessel.

THE VOYAGE TO ANNWN

In his god-form, Bran is recognizably a type of the "otherworldly host" – a being who feasts heroes in his magic hall, feeding them from an inexhaustible cauldron that "will not boil the food of a coward." We can see another example of this type of vessel and incidentally complete the connections between the various cauldrons and the Grail by looking at another poem attributed to Taliesin. He was present at the Entertainment of the Noble Head and was himself one of the Cauldron-born, an initiate of the sacred vessel. His poem "Preiddeu Annwn" ("Spoils of the In-world"), which can be dated to the ninth century CE in its present form, but is acknowledged to contain material from a far older time, begins thus:

> *Since my song resounded in the turning Caer,*
> *I am pre-eminent. My first song*
> *Was of the Cauldron itself.*
> *Nine maidens warmed it with their breath –*
> *Of what nature was it?*
> *Pearls were about its rim,*
> *Nor would it boil a coward's portion.*
> *Lleminawg thrust his flashing sword*
> *Deep within it;*
> *And before dark gates, a light was lifted.*
> *When we went with Arthur – a mighty labour –*
> *Save only seven, none returned from Caer Fedwydd.*

Pre-eminent am I
Since my song resounded
In the four-square city,
The Island of the Strong Door.
The light was dim and mixed with darkness,
Though bright wine was set before us.
Three shiploads of Prydwen went with Arthur –
Save only seven, none returned from Caer Rigor.

Here is a description of a raid on the otherworld led by Arthur to steal the magical cauldron of Pen Annwn. The word pen ("head") refers to the otherworldly King Arawn, who was the head or chieftain of Annwn and possessed a cauldron of incalculable power. It is possible that by calling him Pen Annwn, Taliesin is making a connection with the head of Bran and even with another head, one that floats in a shallow dish of blood in a story to which we shall refer shortly. As in the later Grail quest, the task is not an easy one. Only seven men – the same number as returned with Bran from Ireland – come back with Arthur. One of them is Taliesin who tells the tale. And note that the description of the "caers" through which the heroes must pass in order to reach Arawn's hall, are reminiscent of the island described in Taliesin's other poem (called Caer Siddi) and of the island of Gwales in "Branwen." Indeed, the voyage of Bran to Ireland seems to have been modeled on the "Spoils of Annwn" and may at one time have revolved simply around this voyage before the story of Branwen's adventures was grafted onto it.

It is from this point onward that a more precise location for the sacred vessel begins to emerge. The imagery of this was to develop first into a castle and later into a temple as the medieval Grail romancers sought for clues to the origin of the sacred vessel.

KEEPER OF THE HALLOWS

If the Grail now had a home then it also required a guardian – someone who would watch over it and protect it from those who might seek to destroy it or use it for their own ends. This is a theme that becomes central in the later Grail stories, but evidence suggests that Bran and Arthur are the earliest earthly keepers of the sacred vessel.

We have already seen how Bran commanded that his head was to be buried beneath the White Mount in London. This establishes him as a guardian of the land who is interred within it – a common theme in Celtic literature and tradition. Later we are told that Arthur had the head disinterred, declaring that none but he should defend the island of Britain. Bran's name, which means "raven," is also linked to Arthur, who in folk tradition is said to have

The resident ravens at the Tower of London, England, still represent the guardianship of Bran.

taken the form of a chough, a type of raven, after his death. To this day, ravens frequent the Tower of London, which stands on the White Mount, and it is widely believed that if they ever depart, the country will fall – which is why even today the precaution is taken of clipping their wings to make them unable to fly!

THE SLEEPING TITAN

Bran's wound in the thigh suggests that he is a prototype of the Wounded King who watches over the Grail. His guardianship of the cauldron and ultimately of Britain, further identify him as a type of *genius loci*, a spirit of place such as Arthur later became, sleeping beneath the land until he is needed to reaffirm his lordship. Another such figure from Greek mythology who shares these attributes as well as Bran's gigantic stature is Cronos, the god of time who fathers Zeus. The first-century Greek author Plutarch gives us a vivid image of this god, who is pictured sleeping beneath an island off the coast of Britain, and suggests a far deeper connection between the two figures. The quotation, from a work entitled *The Face of the Moon*, tells us how:

> *The natives [of Britain] have a story that in one of these [islands] Cronos has been confined by Zeus, but that he, having a son as a gaoler, is left*

sovereign lord of those islands ... Cronos himself sleeps within a deep cave resting on rock which looks like gold ... birds fly in at the topmost part of the rock, and bare him ambrosia, and the whole island is pervaded by the fragrance shed from the rock.[106]

This drawing by Sir Edward Burne-Jones depicts Cronos, the ancient god of time. He was later identified with the Celtic Bran.

Not only is this astonishingly reminiscent of later descriptions of the aged Grail king kept alive by a holy wafer brought to him by a dove from heaven, but it also reminds us of the island on which Bran resides with the Company of the Noble Head and the birds of Rhiannon. According to Greek myth, Cronos is the last of the Titans, who, having castrated his father Uranus, becomes lord of the world. He later consumed all the children of his wife, Rhea, except Zeus, who finally overthrew him and chained him in the Islands of the Blessed, believed to be Britain. He is thereafter seen as ruling over a lost Golden Age, much as Bran (also "the Blessed") during the Entertainment of the Noble Head. Both sleep beneath the land, guardians of a door between the human world and the otherworld – the source of all life. Both are wounded, Bran in the thigh, while Cronos is castrated. Both influenced the role of the guardian of the Grail in medieval texts.

What more appropriate figure than Cronos, now renamed Bran, should be the guardian or possessor of a vessel that can bring the dead to life, give wisdom to the foolish, and food to the bravest of the brave? These are true archetypes, which presage the meaning of the Grail and offer important clues into its true meaning.

THE HEAD IN THE DISH

The attribution of the word "pen" (meaning "head"), to both Bran and Arawn would have put the storyteller in mind of other, older stories concerning oracular heads, of which there were a number in Celtic mythology – hardly surprising in a race that treated the severed head as a cult object.

There is another story concerning a severed head that influences the shape of the Grail myths powerfully – the story of "Peredur," also found in *The Mabinogion*. Though controversy still rages over the actual date and provenance of this text, it is clear that while it was not written down until the Middle Ages, it contains material from a far earlier time than the medieval romances of the Grail, several of which follow the structure of "Peredur" in some detail. Chrétien's Grail story would have been different had this older tale not existed.

Brought up in woodland seclusion by his mother, Peredur grew up in ignorance of arms. On seeing some of Arthur's knights, he vowed to follow them to Arthur's court where he, too, would become a warrior. His mother gave him misleading advice that caused him to seem boorish. At court he defended Queen Gwenhwyfar's honor and rescued her gold cup when this was stolen by a strange knight. After a sojourn with an uncle, where he tested his strength with a sword that broke and was miraculously reunited again, he met a second uncle, who is called the Wounded King. Following advice given him by his mother, he forbears to ask what was happening when a curious procession entered the hall. He saw a spear dripping blood and a head floating in a dish of blood but remained silent, an act for which he was later rebuked, since had he asked, both the land and the Wounded King would have been healed. In the adventures that followed, Peredur was enamored of a beautiful woman, learned arms from the Nine Witches of Gloucester, slayed a serpent, and gained the ring it guarded. He overcame a giant, killed another serpent, and won the gold-granting stone it guarded. Finally, he came upon the otherworldly Woman of the Mound, who gave him a ring of invisibility that helped him overcome a third monster.

Eventually he came to the Castle of Wonders where the Grail was kept. Here he learned that many of the characters within the story were his own cousins who adopted various disguises in order to test him. The head in the dish was revealed to have belonged to another cousin. Finally, with the help of Arthur, Peredur defeated the Witches of Gloucester, who had caused all of these enchantments.

Here, the sacred object is a dish, and instead of containing spiritual food, it bears the severed human head of Peredur's cousin, whom he seeks to avenge. Although at one level this turns the story into a quest for vengeance, the Celtic obsession with the human head should not be forgotten. In the story of Bran, the head became an object of reverence, which magically provided entertainment and wisdom for the whole company, just as the Grail was to become of central importance to the company of the Round Table.

Talismanic objects abound in this story. In addition to the spear that drips blood and the head in the dish, there is also the ring guarded by the serpent of the mound, the ring given to Peredur by the Woman of the Mound, another ring he takes from a character called the Maiden of the Tent. There is also the cup stolen from Guinevere and later restored to her, a magical chessboard, and a unicorn's head acquired by Peredur for the empress of Constantinople.

This list can be matched with a catalogue of "the 13 Treasures of the Island of Britain,"[7] which tradition ascribes to the guardianship of Merlin, who keeps them on an island not unlike that in the "Spoils of Annwn" and "Branwen." The significance of these objects will be examined below; for the moment a closer look at the nature of the island that appears in the majority of the texts will provide a further analogy to the home of the Grail.

THE FORBIDDEN DOOR

In the tale of "Branwen" on the island of Gwales the birds of Rhiannon sang to the company, and as long as no one opened a forbidden door all would be well. The birds of Rhiannon belonged to the goddess of that name. They sang so sweetly that those who heard them no longer noticed the passage of time or felt any sorrow or fear. That these were otherworldly sirens is clear, as is the fact that it was they rather than the presence of Bran's head that kept the company in a state of suspended life.

A thirteenth-century Grail text called *Perlesvaus*,[13] one of the most mystical of the medieval accounts of the Grail, combines several elements from "Branwen," "The Spoils of Annwn," and the description of Caer Siddi in Taliesin's poem. In this text the Grail-seekers visit the Island of Ageless Elders, where they encounter two white-haired men sitting beside a fountain in the shade of a tree. Despite their white hair and beards these men seem young. The heroes go into a wonderful hall where they see:

the richest tables of gold and ivory [they] had ever seen. One of the masters sounded a gong three times, and into the hall came 33 men, all in one company; they were dressed in white ... and they all seemed to be 32 years old.[13]

The expulsion from paradise, as shown in this nineteenth-century woodcut by Gustave Doré, underlies much of the mystery of the Grail.

As the company sit at the tables, a golden crown on a chain descends from above, and a pit opens in the middle of the hall from which issues terrible cries and sounds of lamenting. At this, the rest of the company also begin to weep.

What is it that casts a shadow over this paradisal realm? In *Perlesvaus* we are told that the wondrous hall is built above a pit of lamenting souls who are there to remind us of the state of fallen humanity. In "Branwen," all is well with the company until one of their number decides to open the forbidden door. The result is the same: memories of old sorrows return to overshadow the idyllic life on the island.

Both stories either derive directly from or foreshadow the Christian idea of the Fall of man. The knowledge that comes from opening the forbidden door, like that which comes from eating of the fruit of the Tree of Good and Evil, is the same – sorrow and dismissal from paradise. Yet this is part of the lot of humanity that they could not stay in paradise while remaining ignorant of the true nature of creation. The Grail story also reminds us of what we have lost and offers a way back to that sense of completeness that comes from being at one with the source of all life.

Once again there is the sacred vessel – Krater, cauldron or Grail – that acts as a means of connection between the ordinary and the divine. We are also reminded that such a connection may bring about longings for a paradisal state of being from which we are outcast. This is a theme we shall encounter again and in the process discover that humanity did not leave paradise alone – a figure of great importance left with the fallen.

THE ISLAND OF WONDERS

Another late text makes the symbolism of the exile from paradise even clearer. *Sone de Nausay*[74] is a medieval story dating from the eleventh century, but which contains material from a significantly earlier period. The adventures of the brave knight Sone, who takes service with the king of Norway, are related. Most of the story is not relevant here, but one episode is of vital importance for the clues it offers both to the identity of the mysterious island mentioned by Taliesin and the author of *Perlesvaus*, and its place in the Grail mysteries.

In order to receive the strength necessary to overcome a gigantic warrior, Sone travels to the mysterious island of Galosche, where he finds a beautiful castle with a tower at each of the four corners, and in the center a great hall. Curiously, the castle

is inhabited by monks rather than soldiers, and there are two wondrous relics kept there: the uncorrupted body of Joseph of Arimathea and the Grail itself. These sacred objects are shown to Sone, and the story of the vessel is told. Long after having succeeded in his adventure, Sone returns to the island to be married and is permitted to carry the Grail in procession with the spear, a piece of the True Cross, and a candle originally carried by the angel of the Annunciation.

The description of the island of Galosche (Wales/Gwales) is typical of the later depictions of the Grail castle and of the turning island and the four-cornered city described in the "Preiddeu Annwn."

Between them these texts shuffle several elements of the emerging Grail myth – the mysterious island and the uncorrupted body of a great man, Joseph or Bran, and the presence of several sacred objects. The seven followers of Bran have become 12 in both *Sone de Nausay* and *Perlesvaus*, where there are 12 monks and 12 ageless elders, respectively. But the influence of the earlier story is seen in the ageless men of the latter text, as well as the echoes of the sorrowing Company of the Noble Head in "Branwen," the weeping monks in *Sone*, and the sorrowful souls in the pit on the Island of Ageless Elders.

THE FOUR HALLOWS

A modern painting of the Hallows by Miranda Gray shows the Grail accompanied by three other sacred objects: a spear, a sword, and a magical chessboard.

Around this time in the eleventh century a major shift in the depiction of the sacred vessel takes place. Until now it is always referred to as a single object – cauldron or Krater or cup – now suddenly, as we have seen in the story of Sone, it becomes associated with other holy objects – hallows or holy things – which share the attributes of the Grail among them.

Four ancient hallows are documented in Celtic tradition. They predate the medieval Grail texts by several hundred years, but they are still recognizable as the prototypes from which the later sacred objects spring. These Celtic hallows are listed in a medieval Irish text known as the *Lebor Gabala Erenn*, otherwise known as *The Book of Invasions*. This text, which gathers together a huge body of earlier material, contains many fragments of arcane lore. The passage in question refers to the Tuatha de Danaan, a tribe of godlike beings who are, interestingly, said to have originated from Greece. The passage in question lists four cities from which they came and four objects that derive from those cities:

The four cities in which they dwelled were named Failias, Goirias, Findias, and Murias. From Failias came the Lia Fail, which cried out whenever a true King of Ireland stepped upon it. From Goiras came the Spear of Lug – whoever carried it won every battle in which he fought. From Findias came the Sword of Nuada – once it was drawn from its scabbard no one could resist it, and all died that it touched because of its venom. From Murias came the Cauldron of the Dagda – no company came from it unsatisfied. There were four sages in those four cities: Morfessa who was in Failias, Esras in Goiras, Uscias in Findias, Semias in Murias. These four taught the Tuatha wisdom and knowledge.[76]

A whole new landscape of sacred objects is opened up – each in its own place, each guarded by a wise and knowledgeable being. Not only is there another cauldron – belonging to the great father-god Dagda – but also the spear of the hero Lug, the sword of Nuada – more godlike beings from Irish myth – and the Lia Fail, a stone that cries out when a true Irish king steps upon it.

Each of these objects has its own history, which is too vast to examine here in detail. The spear is associated with air, the sword with fire, the cauldron with water, and the stone with earth – thus constituting the four elements. Between them, they can give and take life, offer endless amounts of food, and distinguish a true king from a false one. Indeed, they account for all the essential aspects of the sacred vessel. Henceforward, as the stories of the Grail begin to assume the form with which we are most familiar, the vessel itself is almost always accompanied by three other hallows – a sword, a spear, and a stone. These objects are first brought together here in the mythology of ancient Ireland.

When this evidence is put together, a picture begins to emerge of a sacred island, a type of paradise with four towers or castles, one at each corner. Here the four hallows are to be found. All who sit down to eat in this place are fed with the food they most desire. In some mysterious way, this place is the heart-center of both land and people, even though it is often situated on an island off the coast of the mainland. Here opposites are reconciled and harmony reigns, as it must always in the presence of the sacred vessel. All of these aspects appear in the developing history of the Grail from here onward.

MAIDENS OF THE WELLS

Celtic literature and tradition continued to be a powerful influence on the developing Grail myths throughout the Middle Ages, and many of the primary themes within the cycles of stories can be traced back to these early beginnings. One final thread in the tapestry needs to be considered. This is a text that, despite being dated to the twelfth century, betrays an earlier origin in oral tradition. Enshrined within it is the last vestige of a theme that is immemorially ancient and that not only takes the idea of the sacred vessel into new areas, but also foreshadows the later medieval stories of the Grail.

Written in Old French under the title *Elucidation de l'hystoire du Graal*, it has been dated to somewhere between 1220 and 1225. Essentially it presents itself as a prequel to the more famous twelfth-century poem by Chrétien de Troyes, *Le Conte du Graal* (*The Story of the Grail*), which is considered one of the premier sources for all later Grail romances. In fact, the *Elucidation* neither elucidates nor indeed connects to the later poem at all. It is a curious and sometimes confusing work, which has nonetheless succeeded in preserving a far earlier story of the Grail than most of its successors. The author, who calls himself Master Blihis, tells how the rich country of Logres (Britain) came to be destroyed:

> *The kingdom turned to loss; the land was dead and desert so that it was scarcely worth two hazel-nuts. For they had lost the voices of the wells and the damsels that lived therein. For no less a thing was the service they [the damsels] gave than this – that if anyone wandered that way, whether at evening or morning, rather than that he should go far out of his way for food and drink, he should find his way to the wells, and then no better could he ask but that he received it at once. For straightway a damsel issued forth from the well, none fairer need he seek, bearing in her hand a cup of gold … and right fair welcome he received at the well.*[35]

This custom continued for some time, until the reign of King Amangons, whose duty was to protect the maidens, but who was evil and craven-hearted. He rapes one of the women and carries off the golden cup from which she offered sustenance to travellers, henceforward using it for himself as though it was a trophy. From that time onward the maiden never served anyone else who came there in search of food, and the other damsels remained invisible. Following King Amangons' evil act, many other damsels of the wells were raped by his knights, who carried off their golden cups until there were no cups or damsels left to serve passing travellers. The results of this were plain to see:

> *In such a way was the Kingdom laid waste that from thenceforward was no tree leafy. The meadows and flowers were dried up and the waters were shrunken, and no man might then find the Court of the Rich Fisherman, which was wont to make within the land a glittering glory of gold and silver, ermine and minaver, rich palls of sendal, meats and stuffs, falcons gentle and merlins and tercels and sparrow-hawks and falcons peregrine.*[35]

As long as this court was present, the whole of the land flourished, but when it was lost, the kingdom foundered, an idea that harks back to the period of the Entertainment of the Noble Head and to the wasting of the land after the Grail king is wounded. So matters continue until Arthur's time, when the Knights of the Round Table hear the story of the maidens and at once determine to discover both the wells and the Court of the Rich Fisherman for themselves. They set forth into the forest and there discover a marvelous thing: the descendants of the damsels who were raped by Amangons and his men are still living there. One of them, a knight named Blihos Blihiris (a name curiously similar to that of the supposed author of the work), is a great storyteller, and he tells the whole saga from beginning to end. Arthur's knights are angered and swear to recover the wells and the court "from whence shall come the joy with which the land shall again be made bright":

Sacred wells, like *St. Gwynfaen's Well on Holy Island, feature as places of great power in the Grail stories.*

> *Right stoutly they sought the Court of the Rich Fisherman, who knew much of necromancy, and could change his appearance a hundred times, in such wise that those who knew him in one guise would not recognize him in another. Gawain found the court in Arthur's time, as shall be told in full, and of the joy that came about as a result.*[35]

THE GIFT OF SOVEREIGNTY

What is to be made of these Maidens of the Wells who offer hospitality to passing travellers, dispensing food and drink from their golden cups? Within Celtic tradition they would be recognized as either priestesses or, more likely, as otherworldly women. References abound throughout Celtic literature and later throughout the pages of the Arthurian texts to such "faery" women, who appear and lead mortals into the inner realms. But they are also guardians of another kind of favor. In the Irish story of "Baile in Scail," the hero Conn is abducted into the otherworld in order that he may receive a vision of his future kingly destiny:

They went into a house of gold and saw a girl seated in a chair of crystal, wearing a golden crown. In front of her was a silver vat with corners of gold. A vessel of gold stood beside her and before her was a golden cup ... The girl was the Sovranty [i.e., sovereignty] of Ireland and she gave food to Conn.[27]

When the girl serves ale to the company, she asks to whom the cup of red ale – Dergflaith, the Red Drink of Lordship – should be given and is told to offer it to Conn as a sign that he will be king.

Here the vessel confers the essence of sovereignty, the gift of the land over which Conn will one day rule. The Grail offers a more spiritual essence, but the underlying truth is the same, and the women who offer a drink from their cups to the passing stranger are only a small remove from the girl who offers the sovereignty of Ireland.

In the context of the *Elucidation*, these women have been reduced to mysterious and inexplicable servants, their original roles lost in a Christian reshaping of the story. Yet, there are still glimpses of their origins, such as that after Amangons has raped one of their number the rest continue to serve but invisibly, and that all the women are said to "come forth from the wells," making it clear that they are not simply dwelling in some hut beside the source of water.

More important than this is their connection to the land. Once the "custom" has been broken by Amangons and those men who follow suit, the land becomes a desert, dry and unfruitful, where there are no leaves on the trees and the meadows dry up. This is an essential clue to the origin of the Grail in Celtic tradition, and it incidentally ushers in one of the constant themes of the Grail stories hereafter – the theme of the Wasteland and its causes.

WASTELAND AND WOUNDED KING

In the story of the Maidens of the Wells a reciprocal link between the otherworld and this world is broken; a symbolic fracture between the everyday and the sacred that is still felt today. In Celtic tradition, the king and the land are so closely related that when one falls sick, the other is affected. Thus, only a king perfect in body can rule the land; if he is maimed or wounded – as in the case of the Irish Nuada who lost a hand in battle and was given a new one of silver – another has to take over the kingdom. This theme runs through all of the Arthurian Grail texts and is of primary importance to an understanding of the stories. Nowhere is it more clearly stated than in the *Elucidation*, despite its confusing twists and turns. Here we catch the last dying echo of a very ancient theme in which wells are guarded by priestesses whose task it was to keep open the ways between the worlds and to give voice to the deeper mysteries, prophesying to the worshippers of the divine vessel who come in search of it.

The ninth-century Celtic Derrynaflan Chalice was, at one time, described as the Grail.

As such, their physical well-being is sacred, and when they are misused by Amangons and his men, not only is the land wounded, but the voices fall silent; there is no longer communication between the two worlds. It could be said that this world has never recovered from the severing of ancient ties and still suffers as a result from the loss of a deeper and more ancient harmony with the land. The quest of Arthur's knights can be seen as analogous to our own modern quest for wholeness, as indeed is the quest for the Grail in all of the stories. The hope that accompanies this – the joy of the court – is surely one of the reasons for our continued fascination with the Grail.

THE CELTIC LEGACY

The *Elucidation*, despite many borrowings from later sources, preserves elements that predate most of the Grail texts that were being composed at the time. It throws new light on the idea of the Grail and of the mysterious beings who watch over it. They are part of a legacy of Celtic tradition that helped shape the future development of the Grail myths, which occurred throughout most of the medieval retellings that followed. During the period that saw the development of Celtic culture, tradition and literature, roughly between 2000 BCE and 600 CE, the Grail acquired a new home and a guardian, became associated with other sacred objects, and became indissolubly linked with the themes of the Wasteland and the Wounded King. For something like 500 years after this, Celtic myths continued to circulate, first in Britain and later in Europe, carried by the wandering bards and storytellers who fled the country after the Roman legions departed. Eventually, the stories they told returned, Christianized and shaped anew as part of the Arthurian saga, but with the same underlying elements perceivable beneath layers of new material that had been grafted onto them.

CHRIST'S CUP

There is no need to reinvent tradition.

August Rodin *Letters*

What happened next is central to our understanding of the Grail and its history. From the distant time when our first ancestors walked the earth, the idea of the sacred vessel has remained a constant companion of our cultural and spiritual development. Now, at the beginning of the Christian era, it was about to find a new expression, which would bring with it a huge influx of imagery and meaning. These new ideas were to enter the tradition of the Grail via Christianity – not always the orthodox beliefs, but through a more esoteric understanding of Christ's teachings that flowed out of classical and Middle Eastern spirituality into the new cauldron of Western theology.

Throughout the Middle Ages, Christianity carried the idea of the Grail in a unique way, reshaping it forever and bringing into its frame of reference a whole new range of meanings and associations. The Celtic cauldrons of life and inspiration were far too powerful to be forgotten, but they could not remain as they were, set in a framework of paganism that was unacceptable to a Christianized Europe. So, as the legends began to grow and develop into ever more complex cycles of stories, the chalice replaced the cauldron. The effect of this process on the symbolism of the Grail produced an extraordinary blossoming of mystical writings, which delved back into the Celtic past and beyond in order to explore the deepest reaches of the Christian psyche. In the mingling of these streams, the Grail found new definitions; its history shifted gear, bringing the sacred vessel closer to the world of everyday spirituality while at the same time making it an object of eternal search.

But there is a paradox at this particular point in the transmission of the Grail's history; it is as though the recording skipped a track, jumping from the world of the Celtic cauldrons to that of the Christianized Grail of the Middle Ages without a pause, missing out the central story that changed it forever. This is, in fact, something of an illusion. Within the corpus of medieval Grail texts there is a constant harking back to the time when Jesus walked the earth and to the dramatic stories that accompanied His ministry. All of the evidence outlining this period in the Grail's

history thus comes not from the time of Christ, but from the speculations and spiritual interpretations of medieval writers and theologians. However, in most of the medieval texts is embedded older strata of knowledge, which were often not written down until hundreds of years after they were first composed – a pattern also found in Celtic literature. Within these comparatively late texts lie a whole range of hints and clues about this "missing" period in the history of the sacred vessel.

Death of Adam *by Piero della Francesca. When Adam came to die, his son Seth went to the gates of Eden in search of a miraculous cure, prefiguring the Grail quest.*

It is, for example, at this point that we first properly encounter the idea of the Grail as a physical object that could be sought. Hitherto there had been stories of struggles for the possession of one or other of the sacred vessels once owned by the gods, but these were almost always the concern of heroes who were semidivine and remote from everyday human life. Once the Grail became part of the Christian mystery, it became possible for ordinary people to go in search of it – to dedicate their lives to finding it, as do the Arthurian knights.

THE JOURNEY OF SETH

Between the dawn of Christianity and the flowering of the Middle Ages the Grail's history plots a varying course through time, weaving in and out of events in the outer world while presenting a detailed picture of the way people at the time saw the inner world. The texts that show how the sacred vessel became embedded within Christianity date from this period, when Christianity effectively mythologized itself, offering stories about which the Gospels remain frustratingly silent. For example, the medieval compilation of biblical myths known as *The Golden Legend*[56], collected in the thirteenth century, goes back to Adam. Seeking a cure for old age and death, Adam sends his son Seth to the Garden of Eden to beg for the Oil of Mercy, which will renew his youth and vitality. Refused this gift by the angel who guards the entrance to Eden, Seth returned instead with seeds from the Tree of Life, which he buries with his father when Adam finally dies. From these seeds sprouts a tree that eventually provides the wood for the Cross on which Jesus is crucified. Symbolically, the tree forms a bridge across time and brings the covenant between God and humankind into another age.

But according to another version of this story, Seth brings back the Grail from Eden, and this becomes the promise to humankind of the coming of the Messiah. He will celebrate the first Eucharist with the same cup and establish an eternal bond between heaven and earth.

This idea is followed up in one of the most mystical of the later Grail texts, the *Queste del Saint Graal*.[82] In this thirteenth-century account the Grail knights sail in a ship made of wood from the same tree from the Garden

Galahad, Perceval, and Bors travel to the city of Sarras aboard the ship of Solomon in this illumination from Tristan de Leonis *(1463).*

of Eden. Again, this bridges the time between the biblical era and the dawn of Christianity. The ship was supposed to have been built by no less a person than the biblical King Solomon, who received a vision of the Grail in his own time and had the ship prepared and sent forward into the era of the medieval quest.

Another legend, taken up and amplified in the writings of the great Arthurian author Wolfram von Eschenbach, describes the origin of the Grail as a jewel from the crown of Lucifer, the Angel of Light, who falls to earth and is personified as evil after he leads a rebellion against the hierarchy of heaven. This theme will be explored more fully later on; for the moment it is necessary only to note that once again the idea surfaces that the Grail is brought down into the sphere of earth from a heavenly source.

Such stories are retrospective and represent a medieval desire to bring the wonders and miracles of the past into their own time. We should not discount the stories since they are a reflection of the way the history of the Grail reactivates itself in each succeeding age. In our own time, our continuing search for the miraculous vessel is motivated by exactly the same yearning for the past and for reconnection with the source of all life that inspired the medieval Grail writers.

THE GNOSTIC IMPULSE

Many of the themes embedded in the history of the Grail derive from a source that originated in antiquity, but was profoundly to affect medieval theology and belief. This is the ancient faith of Gnosticism (from *gnosis*, "to know"). Within Gnostic belief are found Persian, Egyptian, Hellenic, Platonic, Christian, and Jewish elements, fused together in the melting pot of Mediterranean culture that blossomed in the city of Alexandria almost from its foundation in the fourth century BCE.

Gnosticism has been known mainly through the writings of Christian clerics who sought to discredit it. Such original Gnostic texts that survived were so fragmentary that a full picture of Gnostic belief was impossible until the discovery of the Nag Hammadi scrolls in 1945 and the Qumran texts in 1947.[111] These have enabled scholars to begin piecing together these Gnostic fragments into something like a cohesive story.

The Gnostics saw themselves as possessors of an inner wisdom, guardians of traditions inherited from the mystery schools of the classical world. They envisaged every member of the human race as preserving a divine spark trapped in matter. The true God was unknown and hidden, although He alone was the origin of light; creation was the work of a false god, the Demiurge. Every Gnostic lived in the hope of rejoining the true God in the *pleroma* (heaven). They believed the journey was possible, but the path of return was fraught with difficulty because the divine spark within each individual lived in the forgetfulness of the flesh. It was necessary to combat the King of the World (the Demiurge) by whatever means possible. He could be denied by means of asceticism, which denied the currency of creation, or by licentiousness, which scorned the created order. Some Gnostic sects were so extreme in their practices that they earned the censure that was heaped upon them. However, not all sects used either of these methods.

The Gnostics were obsessed with the questions: Why am I born? What is my purpose? How does evil originate? These philosophical questions were the forerunners of the kind of scientific inquiry that shaped the Renaissance and brought about yet another clash between believers and seekers of the truth.

THE QUEST FOR THE PEARL

The descent of the soul into flesh and its eventual return to the *pleroma* is described in an extraordinary Gnostic fable, "The Song of the Pearl," from the apocryphal Acts of Thomas,[57] which probably dates from the second century CE. A prince (the Messiah) journeys from his home in the East into Egypt (the earth) in order to "bring back thence the one pearl which is there ... girt about by the devouring serpent." In order to achieve this, the prince puts on the garments of Egypt (the flesh) in exchange for his own glorious robe (divine nature). He at once forgets who he is, from whence he came, and the purpose of his quest. However, an eagle brings him a secret scroll, which bids him awake and remember that he is the son of kings.

He wins the pearl (the divine spark), strips off his filthy garments (the flesh), and returns to the East, guided by the secret scroll (the hidden *gnosis*). The jewels and robes that he shed at various stages of his journey are restored to him. "But suddenly, I saw the garment made like unto me as it had been in a mirror ... and I knew and saw myself through it." He remembers the truth about his quest and is brought before "the brightness of the Father," fully equipped as a royal prince.

The parallels between this story and the quest for the Grail are immediately recognizable. The seeker goes off on a series of adventures in search of a spiritual goal that will enable the seeker's transformation. The pearl contains the spark of divine life just as the Krater once contained the essence of creation and now holds a key to drawing closer to the deity. Such Gnostic beliefs became embedded deeply in the history of the Grail and probably lie at the heart of the idea that the Cathars, members of a medieval sect who based their way of life on Gnostic ideas, came to be seen as the inheritors of the Grail's wisdom, if not of the Grail itself.

A NEW DIRECTION

The mingling of such ancient beliefs meant that by the late twelfth century, the stage was set for a new epiphany of the Grail. The Middle Ages had achieved their first flowering, a springing forth of new ideas and beliefs in minds freed at last from the sheer effort of survival. Art, architecture, and literature were in their vernal aspect; Chartres Cathedral was still under construction, and complex webs of theology and mysticism were being unwound in both monastery and university. The relationships of humankind with creation and with God were among the most important questions of the age, making it scarcely surprising that a new image of the sacred vessel should emerge.

The cathedral at **Chartres** *in France represents the encounter with the sacred in the highly wrought symbolism of its design.*

Despite or perhaps because of the fact that literacy was a skill reserved almost exclusively for the clergy, memory was correspondingly stronger than today. The ear, not the eye, was the gateway to the imagination; when it came to storytelling there were always willing listeners to wonder-tales in which semidivine heroes slew beasts and overcame implacable enemies in order to rescue and eventually marry archetypal maidens. The Grail became a central theme in medieval literature, ensuring that links with older stories and sources were kept open and, in many cases, given a fresh lease on life in the "new" stories about the Grail.

The idea that relics of Christ's life on earth might still lie in Jerusalem spurred on the efforts to free the city from Muslim control.

There was also a stronger sense of conceptual or symbolic understanding than at almost any time before or since. Workers were known by their implements of toil, the religious by their habit, nobility by their rich apparel, and knights by their mounts and weapons. Although the liturgy of the Mass was in Latin, this did not seem to matter; the actions of the priest at the altar were necessarily mysterious, emblematic of his mediation between heaven and earth on behalf of the congregation.

Factors such as these helped prepare the way for the new focus of the Grail, as did the political state of Europe. Prior to the spread of Christianity, the whole of the Western world had been torn apart by war and insurrection; orphaned from its classical roots by the invading barbarians who eventually made the West their own homeland, Europe remained a tangle of petty kingdoms, each one battling for supremacy.

Yet each kingdom, no matter how small, had its own capital. The archetype for these capitals was Jerusalem, the city of the divine king; mythically, it was Camelot, the stronghold of King Arthur. Indeed, the role of kingship within European society was a significant one; kingship sprang from a divine source as it had from the goddess of sovereignty in Celtic times, and kings were anointed with oil in the same manner as priests, emphasizing the sacred nature of the office.

The further the influence of the Church spread through Europe, the more exoteric its expression became. Yet the inner message of Christ's teachings managed to survive; isolated people upheld a body of mystical and esoteric wisdom. Mystics and solitary madmen were ignored, lauded as exemplary members of the Church or, if their doctrines attracted undue attention, summarily dismissed as heretics.

It is significant that there are no "Grail saints," no officially approved expositors of what might be termed a "school" of Grail mysticism at this time, any more than there is either specific recognition or denial of the Grail itself. There is merely a deafening silence, which in an age of relic hunting tells us how deeply the waters of the Grail ran.

THE NEW CORPUS

The Arthurian legends thus became the chief carriers of the Grail myth throughout the Middle Ages. Almost the entire corpus of Grail literature was produced between 1170 and 1225, beginning suddenly and ending almost as abruptly. We can only guess at the extent of oral tradition behind the composition of these tales. The Arthurian canon was established well before the twelfth century, deriving its roots from Celtic sources. Storytellers such as the *trouvères* – wandering singers and poets who were able to cross all boundaries, physical and religious – fused pagan and Christian ethos with chivalric achievement and folk culture, forming an archetypal world that lived in the imaginations of all kinds of people.

Two authors who were responsible for establishing the new canon of the Grail were Chrétien de Troyes and Robert de Borron. Chrétien was already famed throughout Europe for his Arthurian poems, in which he introduced such originally Celtic figures as Lancelot, Gawain, and Geraint to a Norman French courtly society who were hungry for more. Arthurian literature, or "the matter of Britain" as it was known, became all the rage, with countless new stories appearing all the time. Chrétien's last work, left unfinished at his death sometime around 1189, was *Le Conte du Graal* (*The Story of the Grail*). It followed the

Troubadours carried *the story of the Grail across Europe.*

general outlines of the Welsh story of "Peredur" discussed in the previous chapter, but wove its own mysterious magic. In Chrétien's version, the young, innocent youth is called Perceval. He has many adventures, similar to those of Peredur, but wholly different in tone and detail. The strangest of all is that of the Grail.

Finding himself at the castle of his uncle the Fisher King, Perceval witnesses the mysterious procession in which a vessel called the Graal is borne through the hall and is used in some way to sustain a wounded man. From either politeness or ignorance, Perceval fails to ask the meaning of these things and finds himself outcast to wander in the wilderness of the Wasteland. A hideous damsel chides him for his failure and tells him that had he asked the required questions, both the land and the king would have been restored. Thereafter, the foolish youth has to suffer in the wilderness for some time before he finds his way back to the castle; but the outcome is never revealed since the poem breaks off before the mystery of the Grail is explained.

Here is no head in a dish, no *mélange* of curious treasures, no witches or dragons, but instead a mysterious vessel that appears to heal or grant extended life. It is not exactly the same as the older version of the sacred vessel of Celtic and pre-Celtic times, but it is close enough to suggest that Chrétien may have heard stories, either from "Peredur" or from other material that has not survived.

JOSEPH'S JOURNEY

The enigma of the story told by Chrétien touched the imagination of the Western world, expressing ideas and feelings already latent within the consciousness of medieval man. It prepared the way for a further dimension to be added to the idea of the sacred vessel and the seekers who followed its path. A Swiss (or possibly

This image from the fourteenth-century Tristan de Leonis *shows the Grail being carried by Joseph of Arimathea and his followers into the castle built to contain it.*

Burgundian) knight named Robert de Borron, who lived in the early part of the twelfth century and who may have already been working on a Grail text of his own prior to the appearance of Chrétien's work, took the story back through time to the days when Christ walked the earth. His story *Joseph of Arimathea* is worth summarizing here, as it is more responsible than any other text for a hugely important shift in the Grail's history.

Robert first tells the story of the Last Supper and the betrayal and Crucifixion of Christ. Then, drawing largely on an apocryphal text known as the Gospel of Pilate,[57] which probably dates from the second century CE, he adds the story of Joseph of Arimathea, who acquired Christ's body, and the cup with which the first Eucharist was celebrated. While preparing Jesus' body for burial, some blood flows afresh from his wounds and is caught in the cup by Joseph. After the Resurrection, Joseph is thrown into prison, where he is visited by the risen Christ who gives him the cup (previously hidden in Joseph's house) and instructs him in the mystery of the sacraments: the bread and wine are the body, the tomb is the altar, the platter is its sealing stone, the grave clothes the corporeal, and the vessel in which the blood was caught shall henceforth be called a chalice. All who behold it shall be of Christ's company and have fulfillment of their heart's desire and eternal joy. Joseph remains in prison, kept alive miraculously by a dove that brings a sanctified wafer to the Grail every day; many years later, justifiably amazed to find the old man still alive, the Emperor Vespasian frees him. Vespasian had been miraculously healed of leprosy by the Veil of Veronica and had become a Christian.

Joseph now gathers several of his kin around him, including his sister Erygius and her husband Brons (a name that recalls the Celtic god Bran), and with their followers they depart for far-off lands. All goes well for a time, but in one place where they stay, the host's family are dying of hunger. Joseph kneels before the Grail and is instructed to build a table in memory of the one at which the Last Supper was held and to send his brother-in-law, Brons, to catch a fish. This is to be placed on the table opposite the Grail, which must be covered. Joseph is to sit in the place of Christ with Brons on his right and next to him an empty place to signify the seat occupied by Judas.

The people come and are fed the fish. Some sit down and are gratified with food and sweetness, but when one of their number attempts to sit in the place left vacant, he is swallowed up. A mysterious voice tells Joseph that only one person will be able to sit there – a great-nephew of Joseph, the grandson of Brons and Erygius. In due time, the couple produce 12 children, of whom 11 marry, but Alain remains single at this time; from him, however, will one day issue an heir who will fulfill the purpose of the Grail. Meanwhile, he is to take charge of his brothers and sisters and journey westward. Another of Joseph's followers, Petrus, will be brought a letter by an angel, telling him to go where he wills. He will stay in the Vale of Avaron until the coming of the Grail-winner, whom he is to instruct in the mysteries of the sacraments.

All unfolds as the voice foretold, while another angel relates that Brons shall henceforth be called the Rich Fisher because he fed the company from a single fish. He is to go westward with Petrus and there await the coming of his grandson, Perceval, to whom he will entrust the sacred vessel and at which time the meaning of the Trinity will be made known to everyone. The next day Brons receives the vessel and is initiated into the secret words that Joseph received from Christ himself while he was in prison.

THE VISION OF ROBERT DE BORRON

Such is the essential narrative of Joseph. Possibly put together from several disparate sources, it is occasionally a confused and garbled story. Nonetheless, it introduces many of the themes that remain central to the Grail: the idea of the guardian family, which probably dates back to Celtic times, the presence of the Fisher King, and the central premise that the Grail is the actual cup used by Christ to celebrate the Last Supper and the first Eucharist. It is the first mention of the mysterious "secret teachings" given by Christ directly to Joseph, which clearly represent the inner mysteries of the Grail. The implication is that this is more than the straightforward explanation of the meaning of the tomb, the stone, the platter, and the cloth. These were hardly secret, being openly discussed by medieval theologians.

There are other confusions, such as the apparent doubling of the character of Brons (sometimes called Hebron) and Petrus, who is clearly intended to recall St. Peter, the rock on whom the Christian Church is built. Also notable are the references to the Vale of Avaron, to which Brons and Petrus, but apparently not Joseph, proceed by angelic voices. Later traditions, which have Joseph coming to Avalon (or Glastonbury), seem to stem from another source or possibly from a misreading of this important, though admittedly confusing, text.

THE GREAT TALES

Other writers, notably the German poet Wolfram von Eschenbach, whose *Parzival*[114] brought in elements of Eastern beliefs to be discussed in the next chapter, and a vast anonymous compilation of Arthurian Grail romances known as the Vulgate Cycle,[64] developed the Arthurian background and the mystical Christian dimension to the point where these originally separate themes would be forever linked.

The dangers of such rival myth-making was not lost on the Church, which briefly tried to exclude storytellers from communion on the grounds that they were agents of the devil. Eventually, the Church itself took over the role of storyteller, compiling or composing texts that emphasized the Christian origins of the Grail.

Glastonbury Abbey in Somerset, England, has been closely associated with the myths of the Grail since the Middle Ages.

In these they tried to suppress any pagan allusions they discovered in earlier versions. In Chrétien's poem, for example, the Grail is never referred to as holy or said to have any connection with the Eucharist cup; yet, in almost every subsequent telling, once these were in the hands of monastic scribes, the cup became automatically redefined in these terms.

These writers first introduced the figure of Galahad, the sinless knight destined from birth to succeed in the quest for the Grail. He was the son of Lancelot – the strongest of all the Arthurian knights whose fatal flaw was his love for Arthur's queen – and his character combined both spiritual and temporal worlds. The anonymous authors or compilers of the Vulgate Cycle, seeking to Christianize the overt paganism of the earlier Grail texts, have Lancelot tricked into believing he is lying with Guinevere, when in fact the lady in his bed is the Grail Princess. This device, which caused the saintly Galahad to be born out of human lust, has been described as "one of the greatest moments of imagination ever permitted to man."[130]

WITNESSED IN AVALON

In a further attempt to link older pagan stories with the newly minted Christian Grail texts, the author (or compiler) of the thirteenth-century *Perlesvaus* added a further strand of veracity to the claims made for the myth:

> *The Latin text from which this story was set down in the vernacular was taken from the Isle of Avalon, from a holy religious house which stands at the head of the Lands Adventurous; there lie King Arthur and his Queen, by the testimony of the worthy religious men who dwell there, and who have the whole story, true from beginning to end.*[13]

The "holy religious house" mentioned here is meant to be Glastonbury, where the supposed bones of Arthur and Guinevere were discovered in 1184, and the "worthy religious men" who lived there are the Benedictines of Glastonbury Abbey – though whether they indeed had "the whole story" is a matter for conjecture.

What is interesting is that both the Isle of Avalon, a recognized name for the Celtic otherworld and the holy religious house, stood "at the edge of the Lands Adventurous." It seems that even the monastic chroniclers recognized that the archetypal world of the Grail and the Arthurian heroes stood at one remove from everyday life, accessible not only in legend, but also physically.

A GROWING TRADITION

The spate of texts elaborating the Grail story continued unabated. Chrétien's *The Story of the Grail* soon boasted four continuations, all by different hands, which extended the original poem by thousands of lines. The bare outlines of three of these tales reveal how the mystery presented by Chrétien awoke a brilliant response in the minds of the medieval storytellers, who wove new and mysterious themes into the fabric of the myths.

The first continuation of *Le Conte du Graal*, attributed to Gautier de Danaans, takes up where Chrétien left off by following the further adventures of Gawain, bringing him at last to the mysterious castle where Perceval had seen the Grail. On his way, Gawain stops to pray in a chapel and sees the altar light quenched by a black hand. In the Grail castle he sees a room wherein lies the body of a knight holding a cross and a broken sword. That evening, while at table with the Fisher King and his court, he witnesses the Grail procession and is presented with the broken sword, which he is asked to restore. Gawain fails to do what is required and is declared unfit to achieve the mystery of the Grail. He does, however, ask about the lance, the sword, and the bier on which the Wounded King is laid. He hears only about the first of these things because he then falls asleep, having heard that the spear was the one that pierced the side of Christ during the Crucifixion. When Gawain awakes, he finds himself by the seashore, and the country around him, which has hitherto been waste, has burst into flower because of his question about the lance. Had he asked of the Grail, matters would have been even better.

The tale now returns to Perceval, who fights with a fearsome apparition called the Knight of the Tomb, whom he defeats. He encounters a damsel and asks about a great light he has seen shining far off in the forest. The damsel vanishes, however, without answering him, only to reappear the next day to tell him that the light came from the Grail, which was given to the world as Christ hung on the Cross. Perceval asks to know more of this, but is told that only a holy man may speak of such things. Soon after he sees a beautiful child sitting in a tree and pointing the way he must go.

This is the prelude to further adventures, during which he sees a tree with many lights on it, yet when he draws near he finds a chapel. He shelters in it when a terrible storm overtakes him. On the altar lies the body of a dead knight. A great light shines out suddenly and is extinguished by a disembodied black hand that appears from nowhere. Perceval is afraid, but the next day again meets the damsel who told him of the Grail. She now informs him that the child he saw in the tree, the mysterious chapel, and the desembodied black hand are all connected with the mysteries of the Grail. After further adventures, Perceval finds his way back to the castle of the Fisher King and again witnesses the procession. This time he asks about them, but before he can be answered is told that he must mend the broken sword. This he does at the third attempt, but Gautier's tale breaks off before we can learn any more.

THE TALE UNFOLDS

The second continuation is attributed to Menassier, who is believed by some to have been of Jewish descent. He describes the Grail procession again, after which the Fisher King tells Perceval that the lance belonged to the centurion Longinus, who had pierced the body of Christ on the Cross. The vessel is that which was used by Joseph of Arimathea to collect blood from Christ's wounds. He goes on to tell something of Joseph's history and how he brought the lance and the cup to Britain, where he encounters a king named Evelach and helps him to defeat his enemy, King Ptolemy of Egypt!

Perceval learns that the tree of lights in the forest is a fairy tree, the lights of which would deceive him if he let them, but that he is destined to achieve the Grail. He learns that the broken sword is the same weapon that caused the wound of the Fisher King and that it will be restored only when the evil knight responsible for the murder of the king's brother is brought to justice and his head displayed from the tallest tower of the Grail castle.

Perceval sets forth again and after a great struggle defeats the Demon of the Black Hand in the Perilous Chapel, fighting his way to the altar on which sits a golden cup covered by a veil. Using the veil dipped in holy water to cleanse the chapel, Perceval is triumphant when he sees the altar light mysteriously relit. He goes on to avenge the king's murdered brother, and in due time himself succeeds to the Kingdom of the Grail. He reigns for seven years, at which point he meets a hermit who leads him back into the forest, taking the cup, the lance, and the dish with him. He lives as a hermit for ten years, and when he dies, it is believed that the holy relics are carried to heaven, and that since then no man has dared say that he has seen them.

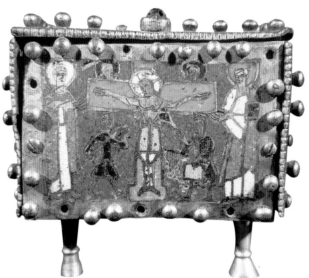

An eleventh-century reliquary. Such objects were treated much like the Grail, as physical references to the realm of the spirit.

THE BROKEN SWORD

Menassier may be considered to have done a good job in tidying up the loose ends left by Chrétien and Gautier, but there is at least one more continuation by an author named Gerbert, and this takes the form of an epilogue. In it, Perceval is given a wife – Blanchfleur, the damsel of the crimson tent from whom he stole a ring and a kiss at the beginning of his career – and a son. The son is Lohengrin, the Swan Knight, who founds a whole dynasty of Grail knights, of whom other tales are told. In addition to this, he writes of Perceval's attempts to reforge the broken sword. He takes it to a forge guarded by twin serpents reclining

Lohengrin, the son of the Grail knight Perceval, succeeded his father as a king of the Grail.

on a sword that took a year to make and that can be restored only in the same place. Perceval slays the serpents, and the smith restores the broken blade, which the smith had forged long since and broken at the gates of Paradise. He is obviously an example of the otherworldly smith who forges weapons for the gods of Celtic mythology. Some further account is given of Joseph of Arimathea's wanderings, including the setting up of the First Table of the Grail, from which the heathen Evelach is held back by an angel bearing a fiery sword.

Following on from these expansions of Chrétien's story, other writers were quick to explore every infinitesimal aspect of the Grail myth. Robert de Borron completed two other works, a *Merlin* and *Perceval* to add to his *Joseph*.[14] Versions of these stories began to appear throughout Europe, drawn into the whirlpool of Arthurian literature. Descriptions of the Grail and of the mysterious procession, some based on Chrétien's original version, others displaying a degree of originality, appeared in Germany, Italy, and Spain. The Vulgate Cycle assembled a *mélange* of works into one great whole and gave an authoritative Christian stamp to the material.

NEW NAMES AND FACES

Into the maelstrom of literary creation fell many new characters, mostly derived from the older Arthurian cycles but with some significant new arrivals. The effect of the Grail on the Arthurian tradition cannot be overemphasized. Not only did it shift the balance away from the themes of kingship and guardianship of the land that had dominated the older Celtic stories, but it also changed forever the character of some of the major players in the story. Thus, Gawain and Lancelot, two of the greater figures in the cycle, underwent profound inner changes in order to make them fit into the newly Christianized account of the Arthurian age. In some instances these changes actually extended the range of the characters, making them more human, while diminishing others. A brief look at the major figures that set forth from Arthur's court in search of the Grail will show what actually happened.

Gawain, in many ways one of the most attractive figures in the entire Arthurian cycle, did not fare well. Hot-headed, impulsive, and charming, he possesses a fatal attraction to women that over and over again lands him in trouble. In the later Grail texts, his character undergoes a decline until he is little better than a noble savage, but he was once the most popular figure among the Round Table knights, renowned for his chivalry and strength of arms, his courage and fairness to all. Behind this lies an older story, in which Gawain was a servant of the Goddess – but medieval writers could not deal with this and turned him instead into a womanizer. In the Middle English poem *Sir Gawain and the Green Knight* he is a splendid, if flawed, hero – splendidly human, that is, and these qualities partly make him such a sympathetic figure. It is more than probable that he was originally a Grail-winner himself, and although only one text, the *Diu Crone* of Heinrich von dem Tulin,[55] makes him precisely this, again and again he comes within a hair's breadth of achieving his goal. He is the first to pledge himself to the quest and the last to give up.

Lancelot, who ousted Gawain in all the later texts as the best knight in the world, is actually of the lineage of Joseph of Arimathea. It was originally intended that he should achieve the Grail himself, and for this reason he was christened Galahad. This changed when he was given into the care of the Lady of the Lake, an otherworld guardian who provided Arthur with his magical sword, Excalibur. Lancelot is trained to become not only the greatest of the Round Table knights, but also to heal the breach between the Christian Grail and the pagan cauldron that preceded it. It is thus

Sir Gawain, seen here facing the Green Knight in the thirteenth-century poem, became one of the most often featured heroes of the medieval Grail romances.

Arthur Hughes's painting (1870) shows Galahad bent upon the quest for the Grail, guided by angels.

doubly tragic that, through his unlawful love of Arthur's queen, he is prevented from achieving the higher mysteries – thus necessitating the begetting of Galahad upon the Grail princess, Elaine. Lancelot becomes thereafter an archetype of all who aspire to the greatest heights of mystical awareness, but who fail because of a single fault.

But what of the three Grail heroes who succeed in attaining the highest point in the quest? They are best understood as aspects of a single character, an archetypal Grail-winner. Separately, they represent individual merits and abilities, which is why in versions where all three appear, they often seem to lack humanity.

Bors de Ganis is Lancelot's cousin and is generally represented as the most human of the three, the "ordinary man" who is married. In one episode he is forced to choose between rescuing his brother, Lionel, whom he sees tied naked to the back of a horse and being beaten with a stick, or going to the aid of a maiden in distress. He chooses the latter and earns much trouble for himself as a result. The act is typical of a man who consistently tries to do good at the expense of his own fortunes, while always seeming worried, preoccupied with the many choices and tests to which he is subjected. In another incident, he allows several women to jump from the tower of their castle rather than be seduced by them – his actions are justified when they turn into demons and vanish in flames and smoke.

But in all the later, specifically Christian texts it is Galahad who is the supreme Grail-winner. One derivation of his name is from the Irish *gal*, meaning "power," and this is a perfect expression of his character. Born to the Grail princess, fathered by Lancelot, he combines physical knighthood with spiritual chivalry. Destined from birth to achieve the mysteries of the Grail, he fulfills every test or sign laid down at the commencement of the quest. Like Arthur at the beginning of his kingship, Galahad draws a sword from a stone, here found floating in the river outside Camelot. No one but he can do this, and he approaches it with the supreme confidence of one who already knows his destiny. Indeed, this certitude is a feature of his entire career and gives him the reputation of a somewhat bloodless character without heart or feeling, belied by his relationship with his father, which is a loving one despite all that separates them. In the texts in which he appears, especially the *Queste del Saint Graal*, he is often identified as a Christ-figure – possessed of the same certitude of action, of a destiny to be fulfilled.

Yet there is something unsatisfactory about Galahad's success. To be sure, he achieves the mysteries, heals the Wounded King, and restores the Wasteland; but in the end, when he comes to Sarras and is allowed to look into the Grail, he dies, no longer able to cling to this world. The Grail is then withdrawn. But is this the real object of the quest? The Wasteland and the Wounded King have been healed, but the vessel is no longer at hand to heal and to provide the inner fire at the heart of the kingdom. Arthur's realm begins to fade from this point – the old sin of Lancelot and Guinevere breaks out again, despite their vows not to be alone together again, bringing madness and ruin to the Round Table fellowship, which is broken for all time.

THE NAME OF THE GRAIL

Each of these characters takes us deeply into the world of the Arthurian Grail quest, at the heart of which were many enigmas. Some of these enigmas can be explained by referring to the number of different influences – some already alluded to, others that will be explored further on – which influenced the creation of the medieval Grail texts and were hard to reconcile. Other problems arose from simple scribal errors. One of the most profound of these concerns the very name of the Grail itself.

All of the texts discussed so far deal with the sacred vessel as if it had always been known as the Grail. In fact, the word itself is a purely medieval term, with no evidence of usage any earlier than the tenth century. The word "grail" itself is simply an Anglicization of the Old French *graal* or Middle High German *gral*, which derive straightforwardly enough from the Latin word *gradale*, meaning "by degree" or "in stages." Though quite a rare word, it was used to describe a shallow serving dish that was brought to the table at various stages during the meal – hence "by stages."

The Pre-Raphaelite painter Dante Gabriel Rossetti shows how Galahad and Perceval were fed by the Grail.

Chrétien de Troyes appears simply to have borrowed this and to have invested it with magical significance by placing it in an unusual context. Chrétien described the scene as follows.

While he is sitting at the table with the Fisher King, Perceval beholds a strange procession. First comes a youth carrying a spear from the tip of which fall drops of blood. Two more boys holding candelabra follow him. Finally, a beautiful young maiden appears carrying a "grail" (*un graal*), which was "worked with fine gold ... and contained many precious stones."[24] The procession passes through the hall and vanishes into a side chamber.

The name of the Grail – and to some extent its nature – is thus introduced on to the stage of medieval literature quietly and without fuss. It is spelled with a lowercase "g." It is only after Chrétien's work became widely known and after the vessel had been brought into association with the cup of the Last Supper, probably by Robert de Borron, that the Grail (capital G), and now always called the Holy Grail, began to develop its spiritual and magical significance. This happened almost retrospectively, and as an offspring of the original divine vessels, the Grail retained most of their original meaning while developing its own particular sanctity through its connection with the Christian mysteries.

At about this time, another development took place that was to have far-reaching effects on our understanding of the Grail today. Some scribes, when writing the Old French words *San Greal* (Saint or Holy Grail) transposed one of the letters, something that often happened in the copying of early handwritten books. This then read *Sang Real* (Holy or Royal blood). This may be no more than a simple play on words intended to connect the Grail with the blood of Christ, which it had contained. However, several contemporary writers have suggested recently that it refers to a sacred bloodline of Jesus and Mary Magdalene, who marry and found a dynasty of kings. This is an unlikely idea, but one to which we shall return later in order to understand why the theory has gained so much credence in our time.

THE OLDEST CHURCH

Behind the medieval literature of the Grail lies a historical fact – the division within Christianity between the Church of Rome and its so-called Celtic branch. Robert de Borron had connected the Grail with Joseph of Arimathea and had brought his hero to Britain along with the Grail. Here, Joseph founded the first church in Britain, substantially before the coming of St. Augustine in 597 and with the apparent warranty of both Christ and his mother. In more than one Church council thereafter British bishops claimed the right to prior speech before those of other countries, solely on account of this early ascription of Christianity to Britain.

But it was within the boundaries of Celtic Christendom that many of the stories of the Grail arose. We have only to look at the so-called wonder voyages, like that of St. Brendan written in Latin in the ninth century, to see the love of wonders among the Celtic monastic scribes. The Latin *Navigato Sancti Brendani*,[6] which told the voyage of the Irish saint in terms that would not have been out of place in the story of Arthur's voyage to Annwn, is rife with elements that might have come from an Arthurian or Grail story.

Celtic Christianity was discouraged and almost certainly viewed as heretical by Roman missionaries, who found it well established when they arrived in the first century. Even after the Synod of Whitby in 664, which established such matters as the tonsure of monks and the date of Easter, all was not as it might have been between the different branches of the Church. Monks and clerics of the Celtic rite were rarely considered for high office within the Church.

Such writings were the product of a solitary, hermetic existence, suited to the isolated island primarily rather than the community life of the Benedictine or Cistercian houses. It is perhaps significant that Pelagius, a fifth-century theologian whose doctrine was that man could take the initial step toward salvation by his own efforts, should also have originated in Britain. There has always been something sanguine in the British makeup that has not reacted well to the Augustinian doctrine of original sin, and we may see in the Celtic-inspired stories of the Grail this same yearning toward independent salvation and a desire to connect with the divine through the medium of the sacred vessel.

This may explain why the Arthurian knights in the literature of the time are consistently represented as going on quests for something that was to be seen and experienced daily on every altar in every church throughout Christendom. But there was something deeper than this. The Grail quest represented the search for a degree of mystical experience that was simply not present in the everyday teachings and ceremony of the Church.

THE TWO WAYS

The mythographer Joseph Campbell recognized this dichotomy within the Grail corpus as a reflection of a similar disharmony within Christendom. Writing of the wounding of the Grail king he notes:

> *This calamity ... was symbolic of the dissociation within Christendom of spirit from nature: the denial of nature as corrupt, the imposition of what was supposed to be an authority supernaturally endowed, and the actual demolishment of both nature and truth in consequence. The healing of the Maimed King, therefore, could be accomplished only by an uncorrupted youth naturally endowed ... motivated by a spirit of unflinching noble love, enduring nobility, and spontaneous compassion.*[18]

This dichotomy is present at the most profound level in the nature of the Eucharistic sacrament itself, which played so profound a part in the mystical imagery of the Grail. Christ was God, yet he is also man. His nature was heavenly, yet he is also of the earth. The bread and wine, before consecration, were merely bread and wine;

afterward they became the actual body and blood of Christ, although they remained, in appearance, bread and wine.

The thirteenth-century Queste del Saint Graal, *the most mystical of the medieval romances, shows the figure of Christ emerging from the Grail.*

This is really no more than a restatement of the very first images of the Grail as it appeared in the sacred vessels of the classical and early European worlds. Each of these sacred objects contained something of the divine; each was a part of creation that could be experienced by individuals as part of an earthly communion with deity.

Just as the early Church labored to define the nature of Christ, so the medieval Church sought to define the nature of this communion. The precise definition of transubstantiation – the miraculous change from wine to blood, wafer to flesh – did not happen until the Lateran Council of 1215, at exactly the time when the Grail texts were appearing. But there was a reason to be liturgically precise about these things, because heresy had begun to threaten the very fabric of Christianity. Indeed, heresies that denied the mystery of transubstantiation, preferring more rational explanations of the Eucharistic sacrifice, existed side by side with an almost talismanic belief in the presence of Christ in the species of blood and wine just as, for many, the nature of the Grail itself was wholly miraculous.

The daily miracle of the Mass occurred on the altar in every church and chapel, so that the mystery became familiar without losing any sense of its numinous origin. Lay people in the West were encouraged to see the divine mystery taking place when the priest elevated the consecrated gifts, while the deacon rang a bell to draw their attention to it. In the text of *Perlesvaus*, it is at this moment that Arthur witnesses the Grail's most profound mystery:

> *looking towards the altar after the preface, it seemed to him that the hermit was holding in his arms a man, bleeding from his side, bleeding from his hands and feet and crowned with thorns.*[13]

Other texts, notably the thirteenth-century *Queste del Saint Graal*,[85] and later Thomas Malory's *Book of the San Greal*,[79] describe similar events in which the Grail heroes witness an actual appearance of Christ. These texts go out of their way to exhibit a similarity between the actions of the Grail and those of the Eucharist.

THE RESERVED BODY

This makes the actions of the Grail all the more unusual and leads us to consider the practice of reserving consecrated bread in an *aumbry* (a box). This happened not only within churches, but in private houses as well, where the faithful would administer the sacrament to each other in default of a priest or deacon or during times of persecution. The reservation of the sacrament is an intrinsic part of the Grail legends and is mentioned specifically in a translation into medieval English of Robert de Borron's *Joseph*. In the episode in question the wife of one of the earliest Grail kings relates how her mother kept the host in a box, being a Christian secretly for fear of her pagan husband. Each day she washes her hands and:

> *The box anon she opened there;*
> *Out of the box there issued anon*
> *Our Holy Saviour in flesh and bone*
> *In form of bread ...*
> *... with many tears and sore sighing*
> *There received she that holy thing.*[115]

Before she died, she charged her daughter to keep the box hidden safely – an interesting example of the way in which women seem to have been the bearers of the Grail mystery, while the men were its guardians, an aspect to which we shall return.

AN ALTERNATE WAY

Overall, the Grail became one of the great sacramental mysteries around which the life of medieval Christendom revolved, though it remained unacknowledged by the Church itself. The Grail's meaning was spelled out not by theologians, but by storytellers, though the essential teaching was the same. Christ was seen as present among the congregation, not just in the reserved host on the altar, but also in each person who partook of the sacraments. This realization is an important one. People did not frequent the sacrament in order to be "good" in some perfunctory manner, but in order to be at one with Christ – literally, in communion.

The fact that the Grail could also offer such an opportunity invoked a thread of independence and individuality sufficient to brand it with the taint of heresy. Medieval people were not allowed to entertain original thoughts on any aspect of faith or belief. In its literary form, the Grail myth may even have presented a dangerous alternative to the available avenues of Christian fulfillment. Later it was to become associated with the military Order of the Knights Templar and with the heretical Cathars in southern France; both movements were stamped out under accusations of heresy.

In many of the texts the name of the castle in which the Grail is housed is given as Corbenic, which can be translated as meaning "blessed body." This is not without significance. Was the Grail being offered as an alternative way to salvation, another form of communion? Is this the reason the knights embarked on a quest for something that could ostensibly be found in the everyday sacraments?

Perhaps the answer is that the Grail legends symbolized people's personal search for perfection, an impulse that could not be constrained by orthodox belief. By the time the Grail romances started to appear, the Church had already begun to develop into an administrative organization concerned more with political than with religious motivation.

When a received tradition begins to petrify in this way, losing its original truths in a tangle of dogmas, it is time for an esoteric tradition to arise, through which such truths are not allowed to perish, but are rather revivified for successive generations.

At such times teachers appear who are able to interpret the inner mysteries of creation. These are the storytellers who realize the truths in a popular manner, and the heretics who delve into forgotten or half-forgotten lore and formulate alternatives to established beliefs.

Each of these approaches influenced the growth of the Grail legends, which could be viewed as simple Christian allegory, as straightforward stories, or as rank heresy, according to the prevailing tone of the time.

Just as there are today, there were then people who made their own journey into the mystery behind the mystery, the deeper truths the Grail contained within its endless depths. These early investigators reached conclusions so profound, they could only speak of them in code and were forced to form secret societies to protect the knowledge they had uncovered. Yet the source for these new interpretations of the Grail was as unexpected and surprising as anyone could have imagined. It was to come from the East where the crusaders, setting out to reclaim the holy city of Jerusalem, found traces of the ancient traditions from which Judaism, Islam, and Christianity itself had emerged. A new influence was about to be brought to bear on the Grail legends.

King Philip IV of France and Pope
Clement V determine the fate of the
Templars in this fourteenth-century
manuscript illustration.

THE CUP OF LOVE

With his own eyes the heathen Flegitanis saw ...
hidden secrets in the constellations. He declared there is
a thing called the Gral [sic], whose name he read in the stars.[133]

WOLFRAM VON ESCHENBACH *PARZIVAL*

Throughout its long history the Grail has acquired imagery and meaning from many different sources. In most instances such materials were drawn into the sphere of the sacred vessel through the desire of individuals to fill what they perceived as gaps in our knowledge of the divine. No matter how this occurred and no matter what form they took, such new branches of the story became so completely identified with the central myth of the Grail, that within a decade of their first appearance they were treated as if they had always been a part of the mystery.

European Christianity, from which so much of the matter of the Grail emerged, also found fresh inspiration, often unacknowledged, in the East. Just as the Church had begun to establish itself and was perhaps beginning to seem familiar, in 1095 the rallying call went out through the Western world: *Aidez le Saint Sepulchre* ("Save the Holy Sepulchre"). The city of Jerusalem, long seen as an image of heaven on earth, had been under Muslim control since the ninth century; now it demanded rescue.

The armies of the West began to assemble in answer to the call for a crusade against the infidel. This was the beginning of one of the most powerful movements in the whole of the Middle Ages, an adventure that swept up many of the able-bodied men in Europe and flung them headlong into unfamiliar lands, where they encountered equally new and unfamiliar ideas. Inevitably, their encounters with their Eastern foes brought them into contact with Eastern ways of approaching the divine.

Out of this came new strands to the story of the Grail, which had accompanied the crusaders in their dreams and their literature and returned transformed. Before the beginning of the Crusades, the Grail possessed a mystical power and was known as a link to the divine; in the period that followed, it acquired its own unique blend of wisdom, which transformed those who sought it.

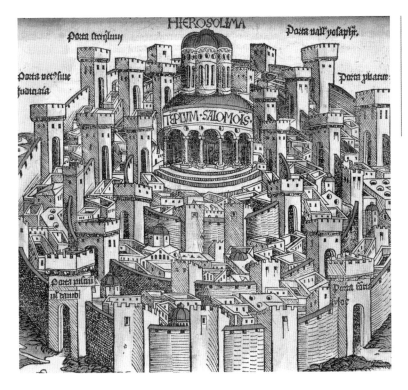

Crusader armies set out to recapture the holy city of Jerusalem in the eleventh century. Here, the city is shown from the fifteenth-century Nuremberg Chronicle by Hartmann Schedel.

THE CALL TO THE EAST

The mythic, Christian, and Celtic faces of the Grail have been discussed previously. Now the story turns to the realm of the East. Islam spread quickly throughout the Middle East from its beginnings in the seventh century. Eventually it encompassed Egypt, Morocco, Spain, Persia, and India and brought with it a new culture as well as a new religion. With access to major Greek writings long before the West, Islamic scholars led the world in medicine, arithmetic, astronomy, geography, and philosophy – in fact, they taught the West.

Jerusalem had been in Islamic hands for a long time before the beginning of the Crusades. Pilgrimage to the Holy Land was possible, if hazardous, under the Abbasid caliphate, but toward the end of the eleventh century, the balance of power changed; under the new Fatimid dynasty permission to enter Palestine seemed doubtful. Nor was it accidental that Pope Urban II should call for a crusade at the moment he did. His motivations may have been politically as well as spiritually oriented. He feared an

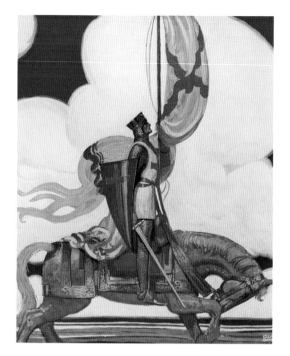

This idealized image of a crusader knight from H. G. Wells's Outline of History *shows how the view of the Crusades changed little over the decades.*

incipient split between eastern and western Christendom, and knew that the effort to win back the holy city required a united front. At the Council of Clermont, Urban proclaimed that he would grant general absolution and remission of all sins to those who would fight to protect Christendom from pagan incursions and go onward to liberate the holy places. In effect, he was offering a certain ticket into heaven; to those who forsook their promise, he vowed excommunication and eternal damnation.

Urban's clarion call opened the way for Christians to perform their duty in clear and unambiguous terms; he managed to call forth one of the best fighting forces Europe was to see until World War II and at the same time, helped to solve the problem of unfocused strength. Christian armies had only recently been persuaded not to fight with each other without good reason, and some areas of Europe still faced the problem of armies fighting across their fields.

This situation can be seen to parallel Arthurian literary tradition. When Arthur came to the throne, he had first to prove his supremacy in battle over the rival kings of Britain. After he had done this, he engaged their services in policing the country. But when all the fighting was done, when there were no more evil barons to discomfit, no more black knights waiting at fords, and when all the dragons were slain, the famous Round Table fellowship began to be lethargic and to exhibit some of the traits they had vowed to overcome. Then, as the whole court teetered in the balance when the scandal of Lancelot's illicit passion for Arthur's queen was about to break, the Grail appeared, leading to new and wondrous opportunities for growth and adventure.

The Crusades were set in motion at the right moment to harness the combined strengths of Christendom into a single spearhead of power. Unfortunately, the parallel holds good when we come to look at the course of the Crusades: great deeds were achieved, but great evils unleashed as well. There are many instances of crusader armies butchering Eastern Christians and Jews, as in the Siege of Constantinople in 1204, and in general they behaved in a barbaric fashion toward their enemies. Similarly, the Arthurian knights who approached the Grail quest unworthily may have wreaked worse damage than if they had stayed at home, since in the end, the loss of the knights who perished on the quest heralded the break-up of the Round Table. Urban's call to Christendom set up a chain reaction the effects of which can still be seen today. Ownership of the Holy Land, the division between Catholic and Eastern Orthodox Churches, and many other issues that still trouble the world today may be seen as originating with the Crusades.

CRUSADER RELICS

The chief object of the crusader armies was to liberate the Holy Sepulchre in the same way that the goal of the quest knights was to seek the Grail. But a problem soon emerged. When the crusaders finally beheld Jerusalem in 1099, there was not a dry eye in their ranks – hardened killers wept at the sight of Christ's tomb. The dilemma had still not struck them until this moment: the tomb, merely the temporary resting place of Christ's body prior to the Resurrection, was empty; their victory was hollow. It was not until the leaders of the First Crusade began supervising the removal of bodies from Jerusalem, whose streets had been purged of every last Muslim, Jew, and Christian sympathetic to Islam, that they began to wonder "what next?"

Christendom retained its tenure of Jerusalem until 1187, when it once again fell into Muslim hands. But, just as no one can appropriate heaven as a personal possession, neither could the crusaders establish an earthly city as a heavenly enclave. It was not long before wrangling began; religious and secular leaders were chosen, after long dispute, and a kingdom of Jerusalem, known as Outremer, was formed. The kingdom remained a bone of contention, as claimants followed thick and fast on the death of any king careless enough to leave doubtful successors. In the end, more Christian blood was shed over the possession of the Holy Land than that of their adversaries.

The Crusades brought many changes to Christendom. Coffers were emptied to send forth vast armies of men, who, when they returned, often found themselves homeless. Disillusioned by fighting and religion, they roamed across Europe, begging for food or forming into gangs who terrorized the land. Those who represented the strength of Christendom were found to have weaknesses: the holy images were blackened by smoke and slaughter. All save one: the Grail, which instead of being weakened by the souring of the great enterprise, seemed to grow stronger.

One reason for this was a sudden increase in the search for actual relics of Christian origin. The crusaders, let loose in the Holy Land, began to scour the country in search of objects that might have belonged to Jesus or his disciples, or that could be in any way associated with them. A brisk trade in such relics began, with enough splinters of the True Cross being brought back to Europe to furnish an entire forest. Inevitably, vessels said to be "the Grail" were among these.

A thirteenth-century German Grail romance, *Der Jungere Titurel* by Albrecht von Scharfenburg,[123] refers to a costly dish found in a church at Bucoleon during the Fourth Crusade and sent from there to the cathedral at Troyes in 1204. This is almost a case of history emulating art, as this was the home of Chrétien de Troyes, writer of the first true Grail romance. Unfortunately, Chrétien was probably dead by this time, but one cannot help wondering if one of the reasons the Bucoleon dish ended up in Troyes was an association with the Grail story. The relic was held in the cathedral until 1610, but it vanished during the upheavals of the French Revolution and has not been seen since.

Even the Grail story itself was said to have returned from the East. Chrétien de Troyes was in the service of Philip of Flanders, a member of one of the most renowned crusading families; he declared that Philip had given him the source for his poem from a book that Philip had obtained in the Holy Land in 1177. What this book was we cannot say with any certainty, though we may speculate that it was an early Grail work. The date certainly tallies with Philip's movements at the time, and even if he did not bring back an actual text, he may well have carried home an account of one or more of the sacred objects discovered by the crusading armies.

Another relic was an octagonal green glass dish, about 15¾ in (40 cm) across, which was known as the Sacro Cantino. Discovered during the sack of Caesarea in 1101, it was carried by the victorious troops to Genoa, where it remains in the cathedral to this day. Some declared it to be a gift brought by Sheba to King Solomon and that it was actually made of emerald. However, there were those who believed it to be even more important. Archbishop Jacobus de Voraigne, in his late thirteenth-century compilation of early Christian marvels known as *The Golden Legend*, gives a first-hand account:

That vessel is made in the likeness of a dish, whence it is commonly said that it was the dish out of which Christ ... ate at the Last Supper ... Now whether this be true, we know not; but since with God nothing is impossible, therefore we neither firmly assert nor deny it ... This, however, must not be passed over in silence; that in certain books of the English it is found that, when Nicodemus [sic] took down the body of Christ from the Cross, he collected His blood ... in a certain vessel of emerald, miraculously presented to him by God, and that vessel the said English in their books call Sanguinalia.[56]

This is something new. We do not know with any certainty which "books of the English" are being referred to here – though it is safe to assume that they may have been early texts relating either to Joseph of Arimathea (here replaced by Nicodemus) or the Arthurian Grail. What is most interesting, however, is the fact that the Grail – as well as bearing the name Sanguinalia, a reference to its having contained blood – is described as being made of emerald. There is another story of an emerald, this one fallen from heaven itself, which was soon to become part of the Grail story and establish an even deeper connection with Eastern wisdom.

THE STONE FROM HEAVEN

Chrétien was not the only writer to claim that he had derived the story of the Grail from an Eastern source. The thirteenth-century German poet Wolfram von Eschenbach declared that his *Parzival*,[133] a long and symbolically weighty account of the Grail, took inspiration from a book by Kyot of Provence, who in turn had it from an unexpected source – an Islamic teacher named Flegitanis, who was wise in the wisdom of the stars and wrote of a great war in heaven between the angels. Lucifer, whose name means significantly the Light Bringer and who was not yet associated with the Devil, was the hero of this war. He falls to earth when the angels who sided with God expel him. Lucifer is said to have worn in his crown a great emerald, and at some juncture, either during the fighting or in his fall from heaven, the gem became dislodged and according to Flegitanis (as reported by Wolfram) fell to earth, where it became known as the Grail. This was all strange enough, but unlike all the other versions of the story where the Grail is seen as a cup or dish, Wolfram makes it a stone. He describes it thus:

A stone of the purest kind ... called lapsit exillis ... *If a human sees the stone, even if he is sick, he will not die within a week ... and if he sees the stone every day for two hundred years his looks will not change, though his hair might become grey.*[133]

This description has given rise to a great deal of continued speculation since the work appeared. Wolfram's Latin is inaccurate and cannot be translated exactly. It may be that he meant to write *lapis lapsus ex caelis* ("stone fallen from heaven"), which would certainly fit the story of it falling from Lucifer's crown. Other interpreters have felt themselves to be on the right track by identifying Wolfram's "Gral" with the *lapis philosophorum*, the philosopher's stone, a central image in the work of the alchemists, which is discussed in a later chapter.

The fact that the impulse behind alchemy emerged in the East and that it entered Europe through the meeting of seekers from East and West who sought to plumb the mysteries of creation, not only fits well with Wolfram's supposed source, but also with the period of the Crusades, when the wisdom of Islam met the wisdom of Christianity. Even if we discount Wolfram's story that he acquired the story from an Eastern source (there is no firm evidence either way), it is equally possible that he encountered it in the writings or conversation of one of the many travellers returning from the East, especially those who spent time in the Spanish city of Toledo, where Muslims, Jews, and Christians rubbed shoulders in uneasy truce, and which became a veritable melting pot for the teachings and beliefs of the major faiths.

Meteorites, such as the one pictured here, were believed to have fallen from heaven and to contain great spiritual power. Was one such the origin of the Grail?

THE QABALIST'S GRAIL

It was probably in Toledo that certain concepts from the Judaic mystical tradition known as Qabala became irrevocably linked with the sacred vessel. The study of Qabala (the word means "from mouth to ear") dates back to the second century CE. It came out of a profound study of biblical texts and the more profound personal revelations that often accompanied this. More deeply still it relates to a difficulty among Jewish mystics of entering into a close relationship with God. Forbidden to mention His name, driven to using synonyms, and unable to make a likeness of their deity, the Qabalists evolved a way of dealing with the limitations thus imposed on them by their faith. The power of God became represented by the Tree of Life, an abstract diagram that represented the entire working out of God's plan for creation.

The Tree showed a series of paths between spheres (called Sephiroth), which must be traversed in order to attain union with the infinite. This symbolic journey represented the course of human life, with all its sufferings and joys – a quest very similar to that for the Grail. However, while the learned rabbis who studied the Qabala did not seek to overthrow the accepted tenets of their faith, they were led further into areas of esoteric speculation, which made their orthodox brethren far from happy. Because of this, Qabalists tended to practice in small groups and to keep their activities quiet; despite this secrecy, it is from this highly eclectic source that the next strand in the history of the Grail appears.

THE BRIDE OF GOD

Exactly as in the quest for the Grail, the impulse that gave rise to the Qabalistic system was a yearning for union with God. One of the most profound ways in which this is represented within Qabala is through the figure of the Shekinah, a feminine figure who represented the compassionate presence of God. She chose to accompany Adam and Eve when they were exiled from Paradise; after that time, humanity is understood to be in captivity on earth, exiled from a perfect state of oneness with the infinite. However, because the Shekinah accompanies humanity, humans are able to approach that longed-for state again.

The Shekinah is sometimes described as the veil of God, protecting humankind from His awful presence. It is she who broods upon the face of the waters when the

The mystical figure of Sophia, an emanation of God, may have influenced the idea of an otherworldly guardian of the Grail.

world is created. She may also be seen as a paradigm for the Grail – a vessel of honor that stands as a covenant for all of God's mercy and richness, a presence to be sought, and a love that prompts mystics to journey in perpetual quest until union or self-realization is achieved. All of this looks directly to the beginnings of the sacred vessel and to the kraters and cauldrons in which creation itself was formed.

The idea of a feminine counterpart to God, or at least a feminine agency within the godhead, was known in Islamic tradition as the Gnostic figure of Sophia, the bride of God. This figure permeates the whole of Western civilization, becoming inextricably linked with the idea of wisdom personified as a woman. The Shekinah was implicit in Jewish mystical understanding, as was the person of wisdom as a helpmate of God in the biblical Books of Wisdom. In early Gnostic thought, as this grew within the ancient Near East and interfaced with the ancient classical mystery religions, Sophia was considered to be a source of creation and redemption. The early fathers of the Church rejected this idea, deploring the dualism suggested in such a theory. Thus, the idea of a compassionate, feminine force descending from the godhead was neglected within the formalized Christian Church.

Despite this, the figure of Sophia became associated with the actions of the Holy Spirit, viewed as a feminine aspect of the creator. In Christian iconography, she is represented as a dove. It is significant that the dove has always symbolized a feminine, maternal watchfulness who is seen as "deploying her strength from one end of the earth to the other, ordering all things for good" (Wisdom 8:1). Nor is it accidental that the dove is a symbol of hope to the Grail guardians in Wolfram's *Parzival*. In the same work, the Grail messenger, the hideously ugly Kundry, comes to announce the lordship of the vessel to Parzival dressed in a hood of black samite (heavy silk cloth) on which "gleamed a flock of turtle-doves finely wrought in Arabian gold in the style of the Grail insignia."[133]

The feminine quality of the Grail – something that was always present but seldom recognized – is emphasized in the section of *Parzival* in which the above reference appears. Feirefiz, Parzival's half-brother, is a pagan and, because of mixed parentage from Europe and the East, is pied white and black, a curious medieval attempt to come to terms with people of mixed race. When the sacred vessel is borne among the company, Feirefiz announces that he sees no Grail, only its bearer, the Grail princess Repanse de Schoye. Caring nothing for the vessel, he is willing to be baptized so that he may marry the one who carries it.

Wolfram's description of Repanse includes many attributes of Sophia and of the Shekinah: she bears the vessel of love for all humankind; she shares the sufferings of humanity so that "her looks have suffered"; she wears a crown of sovereignty or wisdom. Of all the company, only Feirefiz recognizes her true quality. In the baptism that follows, the significance of his personal transformation is shown when the font, tipped toward the Grail, miraculously fills with water. Repanse and Feirefiz marry, and from their union, symbolically a union of West and East, comes a line of Grail kings, of which more will be said in the next chapter.

THE MARIAN GRAIL

Many of the beliefs expressed in the Grail stories emerged from a mingling of Western and Eastern ideas, brought together in the wake of the Crusades. Sophia, the bride of God, who emerged from a distant Gnostic tradition and can be seen as a living representative of the sacred vessel, was not the only feminine source of wisdom and sacredness to be perceived in this way. At the heart of the Christian understanding of the Grail was the figure of Mary, the mother of Jesus. From its earliest beginnings, the Grail had been seen as a vessel that contained some of the essence of divinity; in its latest incarnation, this became identified as the blood of Christ. In the intensity of Christian mystical thought, the Grail came to represent

Mary was seen as the Grail-bearer in the Middle Ages, her womb representing the vessel of light.

the womb of the Virgin, in which the divine seed was transmuted into the body of the infant Jesus.

Mary was also known as *theotokos* (god-bearer), while in the medieval "Litany of Loretto" she is praised as a "spiritual vessel, vessel of honour, singular vessel of devotion." In effect, Mary, like the Shekinah and Sophia, had become a living Grail, a vessel in which the blood and essence of Christ were contained. The Litany makes this point even more powerfully when it calls the Virgin:

Cause of our joy
Ark of the Covenant
Tower of David
Tower of Ivory,
House of Gold,
Seat of Wisdom
Mirror of Justice,
Queen of Prophets.[90]

Each of these qualities reflects an aspect of the Grail. For it, too, was a vessel of the spirit and devotion, a cause of joy to those who came into its presence, an Ark of the New Covenant between God and humanity. It was also associated with a house of gold (the Temple of the Grail), with a seat of wisdom (the Seat Perilous, in which only the one destined to achieve the mysteries of the Grail may sit), and with prophecy, an aspect specifically attributed to it in Wolfram's *Parzival*.

In medieval symbolism, Mary is the Queen of Heaven, as well as mirror, vessel, house of gold, and star of the sea. Her supreme symbol is the rose, and she is queen of the Most Holy Rose Garden in which the Grail lies hidden. As Wolfram put it:

The wondrous thing hidden in the flower-garden of the king where the elect of all nations are called.[18]

Much of the symbolism of the medieval Grail is founded on Catholic doctrine, though it also embodies the recognition of the importance of the divine feminine at a time when the established Church was opposed to this. Devotion to Mary, while never criticized, was considered as secondary to devotion to Christ. The Grail stories gave voice to an undercurrent of belief that harked back to pre-Christian times, when devotion to the feminine principle in the form of the Earth Mother or the Great Goddess was as important as that to any god, though celebrated in secret.

DINDRANE'S STORY

The Grail's own pagan heritage focuses this in the implicit femininity of its form as a cup or vessel. This idea is also expressed in the story of Dindrane, the only female Grail-quester. Sister to Perceval, Dindrane not only foresees the coming of the sacred vessel in a vision, but actually sets forth in search of it before any of the knights.

Her story is brief. Brought up, like her brother, in ignorance of the world, she joins the three knights on the ship of Solomon when the Grail is on board and they are journeying to the holy city. On the way, they stop at a castle where custom dictates that any virgin who travels that way must give some of her blood to heal the lady of the castle who is sick with leprosy. The Grail knights would have defended Dindrane to the death, but she willingly offers her own blood as a sacrifice, which is what it becomes with her subsequent death. Her veins are opened in the manner of the time, and though the lady of the castle is healed, the bleeding cannot be stanched and Dindrane bleeds to death.

Much has been written of this episode. Dindrane's story is unique in the medieval literature of the Grail. No other woman is ever allowed to go on the quest, and in most texts women are actually banned from doing so on the grounds that they are a distraction to the knights. Some have chosen to see Dindrane's story as an allegory of Christian sacrifice; others have sought deeper meanings in menstrual customs or the rights of women to serve at the Eucharist. The medieval Grail writers saw Dindrane as the embodiment of feminine wisdom, completing the quaternary of Grail-winners and representing the ability to create new life. They may also have seen the healing brought about by Dindrane's blood as a parallel to the healing of the Wounded King.

After her death, Dindrane's body accompanies the knights who sail in the ship of Solomon to the sacred city of the Grail, Sarras, a name that probably derives from Saracen, which is situated, significantly, in the East. She is interred there and when Galahad dies, he is buried beside her. In every way Dindrane is perceived as equal to the quest knights, though she herself remarks in one text, that her journey has been harder by far than theirs.

THE LOVE SINGERS

The story of Dindrane is a rare expression of the importance of women's spirituality in the Middle Ages. However, the celebration of the divinity of women did find expression elsewhere – in the writings and songs of the troubadours, who were deeply influenced by the wisdom of the East. These poets, who wandered the roads of Europe telling the stories of Arthur and his knights and singing songs of human love, also celebrated the divine feminine. This was expressed through a movement known as courtly love, which thrived all across medieval Europe from the twelfth to the fourteenth centuries. As well as possessing an actual court with all the rules and etiquette that accompanied this, courtly love was also seen as a semireligious order, a true *église d'amour*, or church of love with its own laws and rules of worship. Thus, a man might look at a woman, might woo her, desire her, and vocalize that desire in endless panegyric – but was expressly forbidden to do more. Actual physical congress was never permitted, at least not by those who obeyed the rules set out in tracts such as twelfth-century *The Art of Courtly Love* by Andreas Capellanus,[22] which may accurately be described as the troubadour's bible.

In this book an elaborate set of rules governing the pursuit and courtship of women was described. Andreas Capellanus, who seems to have lived at the court of Marie de Champagne in Troyes when Chrétien was active, took as his thesis the idea that love is an art that must be practiced according to a set of rules governing the conduct of lovers: who should be allowed to love whom and the ways love might be acquired, enjoyed, retained, or discarded. Love is defined as "a certain inborn suffering derived from the sight of and excessive mediation upon the beauty of the opposite sex, which causes each one to wish above all things the embraces of the other."[22]

To attain the beloved, it was necessary to follow a strict code of practice, which led to the worshipping of all women as representatives of the divine feminine, but especially the beloved object of one's personal affections.

The source of many of the ideas expressed in Andreas's book and by the troubadours, came from the East. As early as 1022, the Muslim scholar and poet Ibn Hazm had written *Tawq al-hamamah* (The Dove's Neck-ring), in which a chaste love was a sign of the highest natural attainment of a noble man. Andreas and the troubadour poets who took up such ideas embroidered these Eastern concepts into a Western courtly system designed for the seeker after love. The Provençal word *jois,* which has no precise rendering in English but can mean something like "blissful joy," was coined specifically to describe the object of this quest, the whole purpose, means, and end of which are summed up in one tremendous line, written by the thirteenth-century troubadour Uc de St Circ: "To be in love is to stretch toward heaven through a woman."[34]

Whether we choose to see this woman as Mary, Sophia, the Shekinah, or simply as the divine feminine, we must believe in the force with which such statements are made and the way that they refer back to the original idea of the Grail as a meeting place between humanity and the creator of all life.

But such things could not be spoken of openly without fear of reprisals, accusations of heresy, the threat of excommunication, and the very real possibility of a painful death. For this reason, the men and women who had discovered these mysteries were forced to refer to them in code. The troubadours hid their message of the fusing of divine and physical love in elaborate poetry addressed to perfect and unattainable women. Other groups were more open about their beliefs and suffered the consequences. In the process, they wrote a new page in the history of the Grail.

Troubadours, such as the one depicted in this fourteenth-century German manuscript, carried the story of the Grail and the sanctity of women across the Western world.

THE GUARDIAN SEED

The soul of each single one of us is sent,
that the universe may be complete.[105a]

PLOTINUS: *THE ENNEADS* IV.8.1

The idea that the sacred vessel, once brought down into the sphere of earth, might not only need a permanent home, but a dedicated body of people to guard it, dates back to the time of the Celts. But it was not until the period of the Crusades that the idea was fully realized. A family "chosen" to act as guardians of the sacred vessel first appears in the writings of Robert de Borron in which Joseph of Arimathea is described as having established a line of Grail kings, who keep the sacred vessel securely and administer its secrets to their descendants.

Before Joseph and his company set out on their journey that eventually brought them to Britain, Joseph received the message of the Grail directly from Christ, who:

spoke to [Joseph] holy words that are sweet and gracious and full of pity, and rightly are they called Secrets of the Grail.[14]

Later Joseph is bidden by the voice of the Holy Spirit to relinquish the Grail into the keeping of this man who will take it to a safe place and there await the coming of his grandson Perceval, the first to seek the Grail in Arthur's time.

And when that son arrives, the Vessel shall be given over to him, and do thou tell him and command him to charge him with its keeping thereafter ... Thou and the heirs of thy race ... shall be saved ... and shall be most loved and cherished, most honoured and feared of good folk and the people.[14]

Joseph does as he is bidden, assembling the whole company and relaying to them all that the voice has instructed him to do. One thing only he holds back: a word that Christ had spoken to him while he languished in the dungeon. "This word he taught to the Rich Fisher, and when he had said these things he also gave them to him to be written down."[14] This mysterious "word" remains embedded at the heart of the Grail literature from here onward. It implies that there has been a direct transmission of the mystery from Christ to Joseph of Arimathea, and through him to all the successive leaders of the Grail family. It is they who protect a mystery of which the Grail is merely a symbol, and it is they who henceforth decide who shall be permitted to see into the heart of the vessel itself.

PROGENY OF THE GRAIL

Wolfram von Eschenbach, expounding these ideas in his *Parzival*, has the hermit Trevrizent describe the nature of the Grail Family thus: "The Grail sends maidens openly into the world, but men are given in secret. This is so they will beget children … who will one day return to serve the Grail and swell the ranks of its family."

Wolfram seems to be referring to a physical succession here, but he also indicates that the Grail lineage is a secret known to the angels. Earlier in the text he spoke of the troop of angels who had brought the Grail to earth after the war in heaven. He adds that the intention of these holy beings was to ensure that "a Christian progeny bred to pure life had the duty of keeping it. Those humans who are summoned to the Grail are ever worthy."[14] It is clear that the family of the Grail is singled out, selected by the highest spiritual forces.

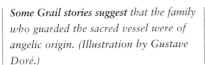

Some Grail stories suggest that the family who guarded the sacred vessel were of angelic origin. (Illustration by Gustave Doré.)

THE GRAIL TEMPLE

The secrets of the Grail were passed on from father to son, until the time of Arthur, when the great quest began in earnest. Until then it was kept in a safe and secret place, a temple where it could be revered until such time as humankind was ready to be told of its existence, shown its miraculous powers, and offered the chance to go in search of what it represents.

The earliest traditions relating to temple-building depict them as dwelling places of a deity, where the creator, god, or goddess, invited to enter into his or her house, may choose to communicate with the created. The earth on which the temple stands is made holy – either through the temple's being placed in that spot or by the hallowing that takes place through the touch of the divine and that in a sense "calls forth" the building as a marker for those in search of the sacred. It becomes, in effect, a *temenos*, a place set apart, where divinity lives, so that to enter this space means to enter the sphere of the divine, the presence of heaven on earth.

The first mention of a special home for the Grail dates back to the mysterious four-sided island of Caer Siddi, mentioned in the ninth-century Celtic poem "The Spoils of Annwn." The Cauldron of Annwn was kept here, and it is where Arthur and his men came to steal it. After this, we hear nothing more of the Grail's resting place on earth until a text known as *Der Jungere Titurel*, written around 1270 by German poet Albrecht von Scharfenburg.[123] The resting place of the Grail is described in detail and the story of its building explained. As we would expect, a member of the Grail family undertakes this task.

Titurel, who is Parzival's grandfather and therefore may well be the same person as Bron, is 50 when an angel appears to him and announces that the rest of his life is to be dedicated to serving the Grail. He is led into a wild forest from which arises the Mountain of Salvation, Muntsalvache. There he finds workers recruited from all over the world who help him build a temple to house the Grail, which at that time floats in the air over the mountain, held up by angelic hands. Titurel sets to work and levels the top of the mountain, which he finds to be made from solid onyx, and when polished, "shone like the moon." At this point, he finds the ground plan of the building mysteriously engraved on this fabulous surface. The Grail temple takes 30 more years to build, but during this time the sacred vessel provides not only the substance from which the temple is built, but also food for the workmen.

The description of the temple is extremely detailed. It is described as high and circular, surmounted by a great cupola. Around this are 22 chapels arranged in the form of an octagon, and over every pair of these is an octagonal bell tower surmounted by a cross of white crystal and an eagle of gold. These towers encircle the main dome, which is fashioned from red gold and enamelled in blue.

Three entrances lead within: one in the north, one in the west, a third in the south. From these flow three rivers. The interior is rich beyond compare, decorated with intricate carvings of trees and birds, while beneath a crystal floor swim artificial fish, propelled by hidden pipes of air fuelled by bellows and windmills. Within each of the chapels is an altar of sapphire, curtained with green samite, and all the windows are of beryl and crystal, decorated with other precious stones.

This nineteenth-century painting by Carl Grunwedel shows an elaborate Temple of the Grail watched over by angels.

In the dome, a clockwork sun and moon move across a blue enamelled sky in which stars are picked out in carbuncles. Beneath it, at the very center of the temple, is a model of the whole structure in miniature, set with the rarest jewels, and within this is kept the Grail, itself a microcosmic image of the whole universe of creation.

It is clear that what is being described in Albrecht's poem is a type of earthly paradise. Details such as the three rivers, as well as the overall layout of the building, frozen and perfect in its jeweled splendor of artificial birds and fishes, all support this conclusion. The home of the Grail is being rebuilt on earth, but it remains a copy, a simulacrum of the true temple. Once again, like the earliest examples of the sacred vessel, it acts as a means of bringing man into closer communion with the infinite.

THE SASSANIAN TEMPLE

One of the most extraordinary aspects of Albrecht's description of the Grail temple is that it coincides in many details with an actual site, the remains of which can still be seen to this day.

This came to light only in the 1930s when Arthur Upham Pope, an American expert on Eastern history and spirituality, led an expedition to the site of an ancient Sassanian (Persian) temple known as the Takht-i-Taqdis or Throne of Arches, in what is now Iran. Earlier scholars had drawn attention to literary evidence suggesting a link between the semilegendary Takht and the Grail temple, but it was not until Pope published his findings that it became known that the reality of the Takht closely approximated the description of Albrecht's poem. The site contained evidence of a great central dome surrounded by 22 side chapels (or arches), as well as other architectural details similar to those described in *Der Jungere Titurel*. Even Albrecht's mountain of onyx was accounted for by the presence of mineral deposits around the base of the site. These, when dried out by the sun, closely resembled the semiprecious stone.

Pope's excavations also confirmed that the Takht had once contained a complete observatory with golden astronomical tables that could be changed with the seasons. A star map was contained within the great dome; and to facilitate matters even further the entire structure was set on rollers above a hidden pit, where horses worked day and night to turn it through the four quarters, so that at every season, it would be in correct alignment with the heavens. Literary evidence from Persian writings, such as the epic *Shahnama*, further supported the details of the site and made clear the nature of the rites that had been celebrated there. These were of a seasonal and vegetational kind and when performed by the priestly rulers of ancient Persia, ensured the fertility of the land and the continuation of its people's life.

Pope commented that the beauty and splendor of the Takht "would focus, it was felt, the sympathetic attention and participation of the heavenly powers."[94] Once again, there is an expression of the desire for the direct entrance of God into a man-made temple, without which it cannot be said to be complete.

From this point onward, the pattern of the Grail's home remains largely unchanged. It usually stands at the top of a mountain, surrounded by either impenetrable forest or a stretch of wild water. Access, if any, was often by way of a narrow bridge (though other variants are possible), and this bridge often had a sharp edge, from which it became known as the Sword Bridge. Sometimes, to make the entrance even harder, the temple would revolve rapidly, as did the walls of the earthly paradise in some accounts and, of course, the "four-square tower, three times revolving" described in Taliesin's poem of the raid on Annwn.

In this place, the sacred vessel is kept, watched over by a select body of knights drawn from the family of the Grail. Wolfram calls them *Templiesen*, Templars, and while it is possible that he meant simply "guardians of the temple" by this term, many have assumed that he was making a more than casual identification with an actual body of men whose history has its own links with the Grail.

HOUSES OF GOD

Not surprisingly, considering the accumulated images that now surrounded the Grail, images of temple-like homes for the sacred vessel proliferated. These "houses of God" can all be seen to have influenced the literary images of the Grail castle or temple. Thus, the Grail became, by a complex and circuitous route, associated with another building, the Temple of Solomon in Jerusalem, the story of which is indissolubly linked with the history of the Ark of the Covenant, an object that shares many of its attributes with the Grail. It is also part of the story of a chosen race and their communications with God, which may have influenced the origin of the Grail family.

Built to house the presence of God (the Shekinah), the Solomonic temple was the concretization of an idea that began with the revelation of Moses, who created the first Tabernacle to contain the Ark and later extended it into the great image of the temple itself. From within this holy house God spoke "from above the mercy seat, from between the two cherubim that are upon the Ark of the Covenant" (Exodus 25:22). But the Tabernacle was never intended as a permanent home, and it was left to Solomon to complete the fashioning of a final resting place for the Ark at Jerusalem.

The Temple of Solomon in Jerusalem became the template for all medieval Grail temples.

Even this remained merely a pattern for the heavenly temple, the throne of God, the temple not built by human hands: it possessed a spiritual dimension, created from stones from the River Jobel, which flowed out of Eden. Here, there is a sense of an image behind an image. The link between the heavenly and earthly dimensions of the temple is part of the Edenic mystery and therefore of the Grail, which in turn performs the same function as the Ark as a place for the meeting and mingling of God's essence with that of his creation.

This can be taken a step further by reference to Qabalistic tradition, where the earthly temple is said to possess two overlapping aspects: one heavenly and one divine. Moses, who received the plan of the temple in much the same way as Titurel in Albrecht's poem, is allowed to observe certain mysteries that take place in the divine dimension. Beyond this is a still higher and more secret sanctuary, where the high priest is none less than the representative of light itself.

The mysteries of the Grail, which appeal to the mind, the heart, and the spirit, echo the division of the Solomonic sanctuary into temples of earth, heaven, and light. In Jerusalem, worshippers entering the outer court of the temple were said to have reached Eden; beyond this, in the Holy of Holies, the dwelling place of the Ark (or the Chapel of the Grail) were the mysteries of the heavenly world, where physical concerns were left behind and those of the sanctified heart began. Of those who went in search of the Grail, few except Galahad reached this point, and those who did were assumed into heaven.

ECHOES IN STONE

The Solomonic temple was to be imitated a number of times in the physical realm, and at least one such manifestation may directly have influenced the development of the Grail's history.

It was common practice among the crusader knights to chip off fragments of the rock upon which the temple had once stood. These they took home as talismans of their visit to the Holy Land and created shrines for them. A French knight named Arnoul the Elder brought back one such piece to his home at Ardres in 1177. In addition, he brought along a fragment of the spear of Antioch (identified with the lance of Longinus) and some of the manna from heaven. According to the Latin *Chronicle of Lambert d'Ardres*,[1] Arnoul built an entire castle to house these holy relics.

It was of curious design, containing rooms within rooms, winding staircases that led nowhere, loggias or cloisters (a feature of Chrétien's Grail castle) and "an oratory or chapel made like a Solomonic temple." According to Lambert, it was here that Arnoul installed the objects from the Holy Land, and it is interesting to note that these objects coincide closely with the hallows of the Grail. The spear had long been identified with that which

pierced the side of Christ and as such had become one of the features of the Grail temple. Manna, the holy food of heaven, can be seen as an echo of the divine substance contained in the Grail. The stone from Jerusalem recalls the Grail stone described by Wolfram. Assembled in a temple or castle constructed to resemble the Solomonic temple, were all the hallowed relics, which also in this instance originated in the Holy Land.

Those who thought that manna literally fell from heaven understood the contents of the Grail to be more important than the vessel itself.

Nor do the links with Solomon and his temple end here. Two important facts remain to be considered. The first concerns the Ark of the Covenant, which has long been recognized as an aspect of the Grail. A well-founded tradition, retained in the history of the Ethiopian Church, maintains that Menelik, a child of Solomon and Sheba, removed the Ark from Jerusalem before the destruction of the temple there. It is still kept in the cathedral at Aksum in modern-day Ethiopia and has remained a central aspect of sacred practice within the church. Known as the Tabot (from the Arabic *tabut 'al'ahdi*, the Ark of the Covenant), it is carried in procession at the festival of Epiphany, to the accompaniment of singing, dancing, and feasting, recalling the time when "David and all the house of Israel brought up the Ark of the Lord with shouting and with the sound of the trumpet" (2 Samuel 6:15). Replicas of the Tabot are kept in every church in Ethiopia, which, when they are large enough to possess a Holy of Holies, keep the replica of the Ark within, just as it was kept in the Temple of Solomon at Jerusalem.

It is entirely possible that this is one of the contributing factors to the evolving history of the Grail. It has been pointed out that stories concerning a quest for a sacred object undertaken by the fatherless son of a queen, may well have reached the

West, where they became the basis for another story of a fatherless child (Parzival) who goes upon such a quest. Add to this the nature of the Ark itself, along with the fact that apart from the *Kebra Nagast*, in which the above-mentioned story is told in full, the only other known source is Arabic, which suggests that the semimythical Flegitanis, to whom Wolfram attributes the ultimate source of his poem and who was also of Arabic origin, may have been the disseminator of this narrative.

Flegetanis speaks of the Grail as being brought to Earth by a troop of angels, while the *Kebra Nagast* tells how Menelik, the child of Solomon and Sheba, brings the Ark out of Israel to reside in a specially protected temple in Ethiopia.

Two further details may be added. We have heard how Lancelot fared when he entered the chapel of the Grail to help the "man dressed like a priest" who was serving at the Mass. Even though his intention is good, he is not permitted to touch or to look upon the mystery. So, too, in the story of the Ark's journey from Gebaa, described in the biblical Book of Kings, when it reached the threshing floor of Nachon, the oxen pulling the cart on which the Ark rode began to kick and struggle and "tilted the Ark to one side; whereupon Oza put out his hand and caught hold of it. This provoked divine anger; the Lord smote him, and he died there beside the Ark" (2 Samuel 6:6–8).

In Robert de Borron's account of the Grail, we find the story of Sarracynte, wife to Evelake of Sarras, whose mother had shared the guardianship of the Grail and who

During Timkat (Epiphany), an Ethiopian Orthodox Christian festival, priests in rich ceremonial clothing carry on their heads the sacred Tabot of the Church of Beta Giorg. Some commentators have seen this as a type of Grail.

This unusual illustration from a fifteenth-century manuscript shows the heathen Flegitanis, in Arabic dress, receiving the secret teachings of the Grail in a vision directly from God.

kept it in a box specifically described as an ark.[14] In this instance, she is permitted to touch the sacred object without harm, but such cases are rare in the mythos. Generally the mystery is too great to be looked upon or touched by one who is unprepared. A visit to the temple of the Grail must come first, and its perils overcome before the revelation of the mystery can take place.

THE PLAN OF THE TEMPLE

The design of the temple home of the Grail is every bit as important and resonant as the sacred object it houses. One of the most frequently occurring forms in all temple design is that of the circle and the square. These can be seen, at least in part, to reflect a polarization of masculine and feminine imagery, a central aspect of the Grail myth. This is borne out by two seemingly unconnected things: a design incorporated into the city of Rome and an adventure of the knight Sir Gawain at the Grail castle.

The plan upon which all Roman cities was based, like that of Titurel's Grail temple, was supposed to have been divinely inspired, revealed to the founder of Rome (Romulus) in a dream. It consists of two separate designs, which together make up the total image of the city. These two designs incorporate the circle and the square; like the four square walls of the earthly paradise or the four-sided tower of Celtic myth. Rome is built on the principle of the rectangle.

r uoit len bien se dieyme saulr
a uil p a tel q mlt miex vaur
c oment Sauuamo abat .j. chli
euant les dames du chastel :·

pur ainssi cele a estacut
uersa setour gualiano
S i quel la gete de sou sen
e t cele dist. garce tes ren
S eplut ren op · i · mot souer

Gawain does battle with an adversary while two ladies look on from the walls of a castle. Gawain was famed for his devotion to women.

The *urbs quadrata* is divided across and across by the *cardo* and the *decumanus*. The *cardo* corresponds to the axile tree of the universe, around which the heavens revolve, and it is therefore a type of the same artificial, astrologically inspired plan as that of the Takht and the Grail temple. The *decumanus* (from *decem*, "ten") forms the shape of an equal-armed cross when it intersects the *cardo*. Within this complex were situated the temples dedicated to the sky gods, the masculine pantheon inherited from the Greeks, and adjacent to the *urbs* or living quarters of the city stood the citadel of the Palatine Hill, a circular form known as the *mundus*. This was the home of the dark gods of the Underworld and of the older worship of the Earth Mother, the Dark Goddess, who held the secrets of birth and death in her hands. In token of this, the center of the *mundus* contained a hole that went down into the earth, covered by a stone called the *lapis manalis*, which was raised only three times a year for the entrance and egress of dead souls, following the pattern established by the Greek temples and followed later by the Solomonic builders.

The hidden place at the center is represented by the ancient Mother worship, existing within the place where male deities were honored. The representation is reflected by the physical organization of the city in the forms of circle and square.

In one of the aspects of the Grail temple known as the Castle of Wonders, we hear of an adventure featuring Gawain, originally a sun-hero whose strength grows greater toward midday and subsides toward evening. In this story, he enters a circular castle, where he finds a chessboard set out with pieces that move of their own accord at the will of either opponent. Gawain proceeds to play a game against an unseen adversary and loses. Angrily he tries to throw the board and the pieces out of the window of the castle into the moat, and at this moment a woman rises from the water to prevent him. She is identified by her raiment, which is either red or black spangled with stars, as an aspect of the Grail princess or of Sophia, the Shekinah, each being a feminine guardian of the Grail. Having rebuked Gawain for his anger and thoughtlessness, she becomes his ally and tutor, reappearing later in a different guise as his guide on the Grail quest.

It does not take much stretch of the imagination to see this as a restatement of the masculine and feminine elements associated with the temple. Gawain enters a circular *temenos* (feminine) and finds within it a square (masculine) chessboard, which is nonetheless checkered in black and white, seemingly a reconciliation of previously opposing forces. When he tries to dispense with the board, he is prevented from so doing by an agent of the feminine, who, in subsequently helping him, teaches the necessity of establishing a balance between the masculine and feminine sides of his own nature. Gawain's own singular devotion to women suggests that he may, as one of the oldest known Arthurian knights, have been representative of an older feminine power.

SOLOMON'S ARK

In this fourteenth-century illustration, the Ark of the Covenant, itself a kind of Grail, is carried through the land of Jordan to the Temple of Solomon.

This imagery is borne out by a further story from the Grail mythos, which brings us back to the themes of the Solomonic temple and the Ark of the Covenant. In Malory and elsewhere, there are numerous references to the ship of Solomon, the mysterious vessel that carries the questing knights or even the Grail itself to and from the everyday world into the timeless, dimensionless place of the sacred. In fact, it does more than this, being in effect a mystical time machine, programmed to bear the message of the Grail through the ages from the time of Solomon to the time of Arthur.

This was built, not by Solomon, but by his wife, who is called Sybyll in the medieval *Golden Legend* and may be identified with Bilquis, the queen of Sheba. According to another Grail tradition, she gave a vessel of gold to Solomon as a wedding gift – a cup that later became enshrined in the cathedral of Valencia as a representative of the Grail.[56]

According to the story *Queste del Saint Graal*, related in the thirteenth century, certain objects were placed within the ship, which was then set adrift, unmanned, to sail through time as well as space to the era of the Grail quest. These objects were: Solomon's crown, the sword of King David, a great bed, supposedly made from the Tree of the Rood, and three branches from the Edenic Tree of Knowledge, one of red, one of white, and one of green, which were arranged to form a triangle above the bed from which a canopy could be suspended.

We should not be surprised to find images of paradise contained in the Solomonic ship, for the vessel is clearly an image of the temple, this time afloat on the sea of time, its destination the country of the Grail. But perhaps the most important detail is that it contains wood from the tree that supposedly grew from a branch taken out of Eden by Adam and Eve and planted in the earth. It was widely believed in the Middle Ages that from this tree the Cross of the Crucifixion was constructed, and part of it was used to make the Ark of the Covenant. The presence of this wood within the floating temple of Solomon's ship makes for some fascinating speculation. The ship, as has been said, was built at the behest of Solomon's wife. It thus becomes a double expression of the feminine archetype, often regarded as a vessel, and sometimes shown iconographically as an actual ship. It thus becomes a prototype of all the traditional imagery of the human vessel, the womb of the earth, and the womb of woman. Mary is a living Grail, who carries the Light of the World within her and the blood that will at length be spilled into the Grail. Within this female temple are placed the images of kingship, sword, and crown, together with three branches from the Tree of Knowledge, colored red, white, and green, which are also the colors of the alchemical process. Read in this way, the myth becomes clear: it can be seen as an expression of the masculine contained within the feminine – of the square within the circle, images of the Grail temple in all its aspects.

During the same account of the quest, the Grail knights voyage together for a brief time in the mysterious vessel. When the healing of the Wounded King is achieved, the final act of Galahad and his companions is to carry the sacred vessel to Sarras, the holy city that is itself an image of paradise on earth. They do so in the

In this nineteenth-century painting by Edwin Austin Abbey, the Grail knights, Galahad, Perceval, and Bors, sail to the holy city of Sarras aboard the ship of Solomon.

floating Temple of Solomon, and Galahad lies down on the great bed that had been made from the wood of the Cross. Symbolically, he is undergoing a kind of crucifixion, part of the frequent comparisons made in the medieval period between Galahad and Christ.

THE HUMAN TEMPLE

The body of humans may be perceived as a temple, a concept that begins in the Egypt of the pharaohs, if not earlier in the caves of humanity's first dwellings, and continues through Platonic and Neoplatonic schools of thought and into the medieval period. To these early thinkers the temple was an expression of the beauty and unity of creation in a microcosm. Expressed thus, it was reflected in the soul and became a means of remembering and contemplating the wholeness of creation, something that could as easily be applied to the Grail or to the divine enclave of which it is a part.

This is the origin of the temple of light (the *haykat al nur*), the macrocosmic temple that lies at the heart of Islamic mysticism, of which the Sufi mystic Ibn al-Arabi says: "O ancient temple, there hath risen for you a light that gleams in our hearts."[1] The commentary that accompanies this passage states: "the gnostic's heart, which contains the reality of the truth, is the temple."

Here we are back in the world of the Solomonic Grail temple, the image transformed and altered, together with that of the earthly paradise, are imbedded in the world of the Arthurian Grail myths. That world becomes transformed in turn, back into the Edenic world of primal innocence, the original home of the sacred vessel, possession of which "represents the preservation of the primordial tradition in a particular, spiritual centre,"[26] the center of which is the heart.

THE HALLOWS OF THE HEART

All temples are by definition incomplete. They can be made whole only by the direct participation of God, who must stretch down to meet and accept the rising prayers of his creation. So with the Grail, which must be hallowed, made complete, as by the touch that makes blood of wine and flesh from bread. The Grail is made whole only when it is full, and it is for this reason the shape it most often assumes is that of the chalice. In the human temple, this is expressed by the need of each individual to reach upward and to be met halfway.

Dealing with the response in mankind to the voice of God, the Word, the Gnostic authoritative teaching says: "The senseless man hears the call, but he is ignorant of the place to which he has been called. And he did not ask … where is the temple into which I should go and worship my hope."[111] This could hardly be clearer. In the quest for the Grail, the failure to ask an important question is the cause of the failure of many knights who arrive at the castle. It is Lancelot's failure, and it is the failure of all who do not listen to the voice of the light.

Qabalistic teaching has it that "the temple has been destroyed, but not the path of purification, illumination, and union that lay concealed in it." For when the perfected soul of mankind "rises like incense from the golden altar of the heart and passes through the most inward curtains of his being to the holy of holies within."[86] Then the two cherubim who stand guard over the Ark of the Covenant (of the heart) "are united in the presence of the One in Whom the soul recognizes its eternal life and its own union with Him. Henceforward the soul is called the eternally "living" [hayah], the "one and only" [yehidah],"[86] the perfect. The light has come like veritable tongues of fire upon all who reach the center of the temple and find there the seat of God in the heart of His creation.

This was the aim of the Grail family, of the *Templiesen* of Wolfram von Eschenbach, of the priest-kings who built the Takht-i-Taqdis or the Capitoline temples of Rome. Before them, it was the desire of the people who first discovered the idea of the sacred vessel and who erected their stone circles to echo the dance of the cosmos – waiting for the moment when God would reach down and hallow their seeking with a touch.

THE FOLLOWERS OF GNOSIS

By the thirteenth century, the Grail, as described in the literature of the time, had a permanent home and was guarded by unique guardians: a family chosen by God to watch over the most sacred of relics. But the Grail family was not wholly an invention of writers like Robert de Borron and Wolfram von Eschenbach; historical events mirrored the Grail romances in an extraordinary way, until it is no longer possible to say with any certainty which of these things influenced the other. To see how this came about, it is necessary to trace a consistent group of ideas that affected the development of the Grail story right from the start.

We have already seen how the early Gnostic sects came to influence the story of the Grail through fables like *The Song of the Pearl*. But this was not the only way that Gnosticism or its inheritors became part of the Grail's history. Gnosticism was merely one of several contenders for the orthodox control of Christianity during the years when doctrines were still being codified. It failed at about the same time as the barbarian hordes swept across Europe, eclipsing a rich classical heritage. The Byzantine Empire maintained certain ancient traditions, including those of the Gnostics; Church and state coalesced to strengthen each other against the onslaughts of armed insurrection and spiritual darkness. While Christianity struggled to make its impact on Europe, using the vehicle of native traditional practices and customs as a teaching aid, the Gnostic vision was borne eastward and westward by two separate groups: the Manicheans and the Cathars, respectively. It is the second group that is of interest here.

THE PERFECTED ONES

While the Manicheans trekked eastward, another remnant of Gnosticism went westward through Bulgaria and Italy into France and Spain, where its followers became known as Cathars. For both Manicheans and Cathars, flesh and matter were seen as creations of the evil Demiurge, in which fragments of original light were imprisoned. Here, an ultimate dualism was put forward, in which evil and good were eternally polarized; the agents of the light had somehow been caught and uniformed in the colors of darkness.

Such dualistic notions were a recurrent problem within Christianity. The Incarnation and the Redemption were concepts that were often misunderstood. The earth and its creations were not a cause for joy to a medieval peasant ploughing his feudal lord's fields, nor to his wife burdened with work and numerous children. For people such as these, respite came only on feast days or with death. Cathar beliefs found a natural response to such a way of life, representing creation as a cause of sorrow, matter as a prison for the divine spark. Food, sexuality, and enjoyment of the world's goods were either rejected as worthless or described in terms of a split between body and spirit. The Cathars sought release from this condition; they yearned for a spiritual life with passionate zeal. Spiritual purity could have no truck with the body, and for this reason the Cathars said that Christ only "seemed" to be born of a woman and "seemed" to die on the cross. Likewise the sacraments, which exalt matter as the gateway of spiritual grace, were rejected totally.

The Cathars had three ranks of adherents: hearers, believers, and an inner group known as Perfecti. These Perfect Ones reached their exalted position by renouncing evil and through abstinence from meat and the fruits of sexuality. They alone could reconcile sinners by means of a ritual called the *consolamentum*, a sacramental means of purification. Its effect was considered final and was possibly not repeatable: if a Perfect One fell into sin after having received the *consolamentum*, all those who might have received purification at his hands were rendered likewise sinful: a chain of evil was released.

Vigilance and a high degree of integrity were key features of Catharism. Often the *consolamentum* was not received until death, when all sin was remitted. Women were admissible to the Perfecti ranks; widows kept Cathar communities, educating children and practicing the Cathar way of life. It was a form of ideal Christianity, but dualist to its heart.

Their plain life, simple food, the laying on of hands, their celibacy, and their adherence to the Gospel of St. John make them seem models of the faith; though strict, they were certainly not life-hating fanatics who sought to subdue all aspects of the flesh in order to attain perfection. They were indeed dedicated to reaching the highest possible goal of human achievement – that is, in the spirit – and to this end they saw no alternative to the exclusion of gross matter, so that they could concentrate instead on the inner reaches of the soul rather than on

Montségur in the French Pyrenees was the last refuge of the Cathars. Here it is under siege by the papal armies.

The fall of the angel Lucifer as imagined by Gustave Doré in 1861. To the Cathars, Lucifer was the true ruler over the earth.

procreation and the acquisition of worldly goods. In this they were no different from the monks who sought God in the desert and donned hair shirts to remind themselves constantly of the evils of the body. Both groups sought to know God interiorly and to arrive at a point of spiritual union that they believed could be achieved only through abjuring the flesh and living a simple existence. Indeed, the more one reads in the annals of medieval philosophy, the more one is forced to believe that the differences between the orthodox Christian and the Cathar heretic were marginal. They may have differed in the description of the God with whom they sought to be reunited, but they shared a deep-rooted desire to return to a state of innocence and purity from which both believed they had been cast out.

For the Cathars, the God of Israel was false, a shadow version of the creator, who had invaded the world and warped the original design, imbuing matter with a taint of evil from the start. In this they show the influence of Gnostic doctrine. Acknowledging the existence of evil, the Gnostic solution to the problem was to take from God the responsibility of having made the visible world. Instead, they suggested a distant First Cause, God, the Father of Light, of whom the Demiurge, the actual creator of our world, was only a fragmentary representation. In this act of false creation, some of the original, primal light became trapped in the bodies of the first men, and thereafter the greatest single objective of the Gnostic was to bring about the freeing of that "divine spark" and its reunion with the true God. In this they had help from Christ, who, although He never became man as in orthodox belief, was nevertheless seen as a son of the true God, sent into the world of matter to aid in its redemption.

So humanity began, almost by accident, with grains of original light trapped within each person, and each grain must spend itself trying to be reunited with God. The drama of exile, which was to be played out again in the orthodox story of Eden, was firmly founded in Gnostic belief. In due course, the Grail itself would be seen as a key, which led back to the original, lost state of innocence, a gateway between the worlds of matter and spirit, darkness and pure light. The origin of this idea emerges directly from the beliefs of the Gnostics.

In various Gnostic texts Lucifer, the Prince of Light, is seen as the principle hero of this struggle, fighting, as his name would suggest, to bring light into the darkness of the wrongful creation. It is easy to see how Wolfram von Eschenbach might have encountered this idea and made it a central theme of his poem.

THE PERFECT ONES

Many such Gnostic ideas were enshrined in the beliefs of the Cathars, who by the beginning of the eleventh century, had established a firm foothold in a part of southern France known as the Languedoc. There, centers of learning, music, medicine, and philosophy flourished, based largely on those of the East, with which trade was well established. Throughout the area there existed a thriving industry in the translation and study of Arabic manuscripts and Qabalistic learning. Eastern medicine, philosophy, science, and alchemy were openly taught and discussed.

The Cathar priests wandered far and wide, consolidating their hold over the people of southern France and extending their sphere of influence into Italy and parts of Germany and Spain. Word of their teachings and beliefs began to reach the ears of Pope Innocent III. They also came to the attention of the renowned theologian Bernard of Clairvaux, who later had a profound influence on the history of the Grail; he publicly attacked the population of the Languedoc, claiming that their churches were empty and that they had no true priests. His words met with a mixed reception, cheered in some places, booed in others, and he soon returned to his monastery.

Dominic de Guzman, shown here in a detail from The Coronation of the Virgin *by Fra Angelica, was the principal adversary of the Cathars.*

But a new order of friars led by the Spaniard Dominic de Guzman (later St. Dominic) began tramping the roads in pursuit of the Perfecti, at first attempting to dissuade them with

The renegade Cathars were driven out of the Languedoc and eventually tortured and killed for their beliefs.

gentle speech, then moving swiftly to the threat of excommunication.

When such verbal warnings failed to have any noticeable effect, stronger measures were sought, and when in 1208 a papal officer named Peter of Castelnau was murdered at the behest of known supporter of the heretics, Raymond VI, count of Toulouse, this was all the excuse Pope Innocent III needed to raise a crusade against the Cathars. He found the nobility of northern France only too willing to wage a "holy war" against their wealthy, cultured neighbors, and the pope was too concerned to stamp out Catharism to look closely into the motivation of his allies.

The Albigensian Crusade (named after the town of Albi, a center of Cathar belief) was launched in 1208. Over the period of the next ten years, thousands perished on the swords of the crusaders or in the fires laid by the Dominicans. Many were probably not Cathars at all but innocent people caught up in the horrific struggle. One of the leaders of the crusaders, the sadistic Simon de Montfort, is said to have ordered an entire garrison to be burned, declaring "God will find His own."

During and after the destruction of the Cathars, a persistent rumor circulated that either they had secret knowledge of the Grail or they might be its guardians. While no actual proof exists to support this idea, there are some close parallels between Cathar beliefs and the nature of the Grail.

THE MOUNTAIN OF THE GRAIL

Shortly before he was to die in the fires of the Inquisition, the Cathar bishop Girard of Montefiore declared that:

It is not I alone whom the Holy Spirit visits. I have a large family on earth, and it comprises a great number of men to whom, on certain days, and at certain times, the Spirit gives light.[78]

Such words could have been spoken by one of the kings of the Grail in almost any of the texts and could have referred to the family of the Grail, visited indeed by the Holy Spirit "on certain days and at certain times," as in Wolfram's poem, where he describes a dove descending every day to lay a sacred host on the stone of the Grail.

Certainly the notion that the Cathars possessed inner knowledge of the Grail grew to become an accepted fact, perhaps due to a recognition that, like the Cathars themselves, the Grail stood for an alternative approach to Christ's teachings. The strength of the association is shown in an incident that took place during the final siege of Montségur, the great Cathar citadel in the Pyrenees that held out longest of all against the invading armies of the north.

Montségur, whose name so closely resembles Muntsalvache, the name of the mountain on which stood the Grail castle of Wolfram's *Parzival* and other texts, was ruled over by the Countess Esclarmonde of Foix, perhaps the most famous of the female Perfecti. Indeed, so revered was she that many refused to believe that she had died shortly before the destruction of Montségur, believing her to be sleeping until doomsday in the caves that riddled the mountainside beneath the castle. Many identified her with the Grail princess, Repanse de Schoye.

It was in these circumstances that the incident mentioned above took place. During the long siege of Montségur, a member of the family of Esclarmonde, the flamboyant Pierre-Roger of Mirepoix, dressed himself in white armor and appeared on the walls of the citadel with a golden-hilted sword held on high. At this sight, many of the besieging army fled in terror, declaring that a "knight of the Grail" had come against them.

Another story, probably apocryphal, describes how the original cup of the Last Supper was hidden in the cave of San Juan de la Pena in 713 (though it does not suggest how it came there) by an Aragonese bishop, Audebert. When the Moors threatened Aragon at the beginning of the twelfth century, the sacred cup was removed and taken to the Pyrenees, where it was entrusted to the Cathars. When they were destroyed, the cup was smuggled back into Spain and hidden in the cave again, this time under the protection of Martin I, the then king of Aragon. In later years, this cup was identified with one kept in the cathedral of Valencia, which tradition claimed was the Grail. Whether or not one accepts this story, it is notable that it was the Cathars to whom the precious object was entrusted. Did this represent a long-held belief that they were the guardians of the Grail?

In due course, Montségur fell; its defenders were killed or burned without trial below the walls. To this day the place has an atmosphere of horror to which many bear witness. If this was the home of the Grail, it has retained none of its sanctity. However, the story is told that on the night before it fell, four of the Perfecti escaped over the walls and thence into the mountains, taking with them their holy books and other secret treasures – among which was believed to be a certain cup.

Whether or not they bore the Grail is not important for the purposes of our argument. If some of the Perfecti escaped, as seems more than reasonable, they took with them the secrets of their faith. For every hundred heretics who perished, half as many again escaped into the mountains and beyond, into Italy and Germany, where their treasures were scattered.

The sun rises above the Pyrenean fortress of Montségur. Here the Cathars made a last stand against the armies of the Church.

But their doctrines and beliefs lived on, and their survival can be traced through widespread traditions of esoteric knowledge, according to which some of those holy books found their way into the hands of Rosicrucian adepts, encountered in the next chapter, who carried the knowledge of the Cathars into the centuries that followed.

Elements of Cathar belief filtered into the Grail texts. In Chrétien de Troyes's poem *Lancelot*,[29] which predates his work on the Grail, the knights of King Arthur, after communion, give each other the kiss of peace, according to the custom of the Eastern rite, which the Cathars took over in their rite of the *manisola*, the Love Feast, which itself suggests both the imagery of the Last Supper and the banquet of the Holy Grail.

The Cathars, with their beliefs in the evil nature of the flesh and their desire to transcend their humanity and to find unity with the God of Light, were filled with a burning anguish of spirit that drove them to the greatest levels of privation. The Cathars purified themselves to become vessels of light in a rite known as the *endura*, which involved many hours of fasting, sometimes to the point of death. This they did out of love of God and a desire to become one with the divine light. It is this, rather than any possible truth about their having possessed the Grail, that makes them one with its universal family.

THE HERESY OF LOVE

There is evidence that the troubadours, who enshrined a number of Eastern beliefs in their works, were by no means ignorant of Cathar beliefs – their travels brought them frequently into the area of France where the Cathars were most entrenched. Evidence of some closeness between the two groups is to be found scattered throughout troubadour poetry. One of the foremost troubadours, Pierre Vidal, wrote a song in praise of hospitality, which on the surface seems innocent enough, but becomes less so when it is realized that all the castles and hospices mentioned in the poem were either Cathar strongholds or situated in areas where they were particularly active.

Despite a surface celebration of physical love, the troubadours actually extolled the virtue of chastity. And, like the Perfecti, they received from their lady a single kiss of initiation. They also distinguished two stages in the service to one's lady just as the Cathars distinguished between believers and perfect ones. Both groups reviled the clergy and the clergy's allies, the members of the feudal caste. They liked best to lead a wandering life, seeking the transformation that was such a central part of the Grail quest.

The one problem that does seem to preclude any close identification between Catharism and the troubadour ethic – the hatred of physical love by one group against its celebration by the other – vanishes when one accepts that the troubadours celebrated not physical love at all, but rather an abstract, distanced worship of womankind – of the divine feminine itself.

Courtly love emerged from this tremendous mingling of the heresies of spirit and flesh, which in turn fueled the explosion of medieval Grail narratives. There is a natural chain of succession leading from troubadours and Cathars (both inheritors of Gnostic beliefs), which finally emerged in the medieval narratives of Arthur and the quest for the Grail. These are all a natural outcome of the hunger for original truth, a closer contact with deity, and a longing to return to the first home (be it Eden or heaven or the otherworld), which date back to the mythic origins of the sacred vessel.

THE WARRIORS OF GOD

A third group, who were no strangers to Gnostic beliefs and practices, became even more deeply associated with the family of the Grail; whether this was due to a statement in Wolfram von Eschenbach's *Parzival*, or to part of a much deeper truth, remains open to speculation.

Burgundian knight Hughes de Payens, together with eight crusader companions, founded in 1118 a new order of chivalry, dedicated to poverty, chastity, and obedience and established specifically "in honour of Our Lady" to guard the pilgrim routes to the Holy Land. This was something wholly new in the Western world, though similar orders existed in the East. The idea of combining the piety of a monastic way of life with the rules of chivalry must have seemed as startling as it was original. Yet little is known about the man who founded the order except that he described himself as "a poor knight" and held a small fief at Payens only a few miles from Troyes, where Chrétien wrote the first Grail story some 62 years later.

Hughes de Payens was in fact related to Bernard of Clairvaux, one of the most famous theologians of the age and the founder of the Cistercian order. It was to Bernard that Hughes wrote, begging him to sponsor the new order and to give them a rule by which to orient their lives. After some hesitation, Bernard took up their cause, and it was largely due to his influence that the order was ratified at the Council of Troyes in 1129. They were permitted to wear a white robe with a red cross emblazoned on the right shoulder and were given as their headquarters in the East the building believed to have been the Temple of Solomon in Jerusalem. From this they received the name by which they were known – the Knights Templar.

From this beginning grew the single most famous military organization of the Middle Ages. The Templars became the permanent "police" of the tiny war-torn Kingdom of Jerusalem; they fought with utter dedication and were feared by Muslim and Christian alike. St. Bernard's rule was a harsh one, binding the knights to forswear home and country and to fight to the death for the holy places of Christendom. For the sake of chastity, they had to sleep fully clothed in lighted dormitories, nor were they permitted to receive private letters – any communication had to be read aloud before the company. They had to attend Mass at least three times a week wherever they were, accept every combat that came their way, despite the odds, and neither ask nor give quarter.

Bernard's sponsorship alone was sufficient to swell the ranks rapidly. Soon the order began to build a network of castles, called "commanderies," across the Holy Land and in France, England, and elsewhere in Europe. Their power and strength increased, and their wealth grew accordingly. Though each individual forswore personal possessions, they gave freely of their goods to the order and began also to win much treasure in their battles with the Arabs. In time, they became so wealthy and of such good standing, that they virtually became the bankers of Europe, lending huge sums to help finance the Crusades. But as their political power grew, so their enemies increased. Finally, the miserly and avaricious king of France, Philip the Fair, plotted to bring about their downfall – for the most astonishing of reasons.

The Great Seal of the Templars shows two knights riding on one horse – a symbol of their pledge of poverty and companionship.

Philip charged the order with heresy and in a single night had the greater part of their number taken prisoner. They were tortured and, under pressure, admitted to every kind of crime, from sodomy to spitting on the Cross. The last grand master of the Knights Templar, the saintly Jacques de Molay, was executed on 19 May 1314, bringing the order effectively to an end, 196 years after its foundation. Arguments continued to rage on for several years after this, but no one was willing to defend the Templars. Such are the historical facts. Behind them lies an even more remarkable story, one that is closely linked to the inner history of the Grail.

The great castle of Krak de Chevaliers represented the powerful presence of the crusaders in the Holy Land. It may well have influenced ideas of the Grail castle.

A NEW KNIGHTHOOD

There are several facts about the Templars worth noting. First, there is the name, which though it is said to derive from the Temple of Solomon, also aligns them with Wolfram's guardians of the Grail. Then there is the connection with Bernard of Clairvaux. As well as the rule, he wrote, at the request of Hughes de Payens (to whom he dedicated it), "A Treatise in Praise of the New Knighthood,"[9] in which he speaks of the order in terms uncannily similar to the Grail knights:

> *It seems ... that a new knighthood has recently appeared on earth, and precisely in that part of it which the Orient from on high visited in the flesh ... It ceaselessly wages a twofold war both against flesh and blood and against the spiritual army of evil in the heavens.[9]*

The idea was something wholly new. Though the Church had long seen itself as the army of God, this had never been taken to the extreme of arming its priests. The ideas seemed mutually exclusive. Yet, this is precisely what the Templars became, priests and soldiers "doubly armed" writes Bernard, so that they "need fear neither demons nor men." Adding that "these are the picked troops of God" and exhorting them that "precious in the eyes of the Lord is the death of the holy ones, whether they die in battle or in bed, but death in battle is more precious as it is the more glorious ... If he [the knight] fights for a good reason, the issue of this fight can never be evil."[9]

St. Bernard of Clairvaux is depicted here in a vision of Mary, the mother of Jesus, whom the Templars considered their divine inspiration.

Yet these men, whom Bernard says will be "in the company of perfect men" (a term curiously reminiscent of the Cathar Perfecti), are later reviled and their order discredited and destroyed. Among the list of crimes, both sacred and secular, of which the Templars were accused, were the harboring of the Cathars and of friendship to the Islamic sect of the Ismaelites, their nearest equivalent in the East. Both accusations are possibly true, at least in part. The order did offer sanctuary to wrongdoers, provided they forswore their former lives and obeyed the Templar rule. The period of testing was lengthy, however, and discipline was strict. It is also more than likely that some of the Cathars fleeing from the south did find their way into the order and may even have influenced it from within. It is interesting to note that the Templars were widely known to accept men with a past and that records exist that suggest a curious form of absolution for such men. It is said to have taken the form of the following words:

> *I pray God that He will pardon you your sins as he pardoned them to Saint Mary Magdalene and the thief who was put on the Cross.*[78]

Galcerand de Teus, the Templar who vouchsafed this, was persuaded under torture to admit that the "thief" was to be understood as Christ (rather than one

of the thieves traditionally crucified alongside Jesus). He added that at the moment
the lance of Longinus pierced the side of the doomed Messiah he:

> *Repented that he had said he was God, the King of the Jews, and having in*
> *this way repented concerning his sin, he asked pardon of the true God and*
> *thus the true God spared him.*[78]

This remarkable "confession" is startlingly like the beliefs of the Cathars, as well as
harking back to earlier Gnostic teachings. It is significant also that it places the
incident at the moment of the piercing of Christ's side with the lance, which was later
identified as the Grail spear.

THE MANDYLION

As if these links were not enough, it has been suggested that the Templars may have
been the guardians of a relic of such importance that it outshone even the Grail –
though the two were connected. According to the theory, there is reason to believe
that the object known as the Mandylion passed through the hands of the Templar
order during the height of its power and that this same object, which seems to have
been a piece of cloth, folded several times and stretched between frames of wood, may
have been the shroud of Christ, apparently lost to the world during the siege of
Constantinople in 1204, but possibly disguised in this form to prevent it from falling
into Muslim hands. This same relic is found in the cathedral of Turin and is the
subject of continuing controversy and worldwide scientific investigation.

If this theory is right, not only does this present the Templars as possessing a
sacred relic, it also goes some way toward explaining another of the "blasphemies"
of which they were accused. This concerned the worship of a graven idol called
Baphomet (usually accepted as a corruption of Muhammad) and described as a
bearded head wearing a crown.

This could easily be a garbled understanding of the Mandylion, which was folded
so that only the bearded face of Christ, marked with the wounds caused by the crown
of thorns, could be seen. Either of these objects could have recalled the head in the
dish from the old Welsh story of "Peredur" on which Chrétien de Troyes almost
certainly based his story of the Grail.

Two of the most important Grail texts hint at this. In the thirteenth-century *Perlesvaus*[13] and the Cistercian-inspired *Queste del Saint Graal*,[82] which was composed at St. Bernard's monastery at Clairvaux, there are echoes of this mysterious image. In *Perlesvaus*, King Arthur himself witnessed the Grail mass, and when he looked toward the altar:

> It seemed to him that the holy hermit [who was officiating] held between his hands a man bleeding from his side and in his palms and in his feet, and crowned with thorns.[82]

Someone holding the Mandylion between their hands and raising it above the altar could certainly be said to be worshipping a sacred head, just as the Templars are said to have done.

In the *Queste*, Galahad attends Mass in the temple of Sarras, the holy city of the Grail. Here the vessel is kept in an ark standing upon a silver table – an image that recalls not only the actual Temple of Solomon, but also the model of the Holy Sepulchre found in every Templar commanderie throughout the world where their most sacred rites were performed.

So there are the Templars, based at the site of Solomon's temple, guarding a sacred relic, holding a special devotion to the Virgin, and supported by St. Bernard; elements that have links to the story of the Grail. Approved by the pope and with a rule written by one of the foremost churchmen in the Western world, the Templars came to represent the highest standard of earthly power for a time.

The whole of Western Christendom had grown used to the idea of the knight. The Templars were super-knights, combining the skills of fighting men with the spiritual fervor of the priesthood. It is not surprising that those who wrote about the Grail took the order as a model not only for the Grail chivalry, but also for the company of knights of the Round Table.

This sixteenth-century painting by El Greco represents St. Veronica with the Holy Shroud. The folded cloth, known as the Mandylion, may have influenced descriptions of the Grail.

THE HIDDEN KING

The story of the Grail family is a continuing one. References to those who guard the Grail appear at odd moments in the chronicles of our history. Among those guardians whose names are recorded, one stands out. We cannot leave this account of the family of the Grail without some reference to him. Again, the source is Wolfram's poem. According to this account, Parzival's parti-colored half-brother, Feirefiz, wedded to the Grail princess Repanse de Schoye, begets on her a son who was named Lohengrin, and he in turn sires an even greater figure of mystery and might.

The first mention of this character, little more than a rumor, comes in a medieval chronicle, which in an entry for the year 1145, relates how a certain Bishop Hugh of Cabalah visited Rome and learned how, some years previous to this:

> *a certain Priest and King named John, who lives on the further side of Persia and Armenia in the remote East, and who with all his people were Christians … had overcome the royal brothers Samiardi, Kings of the Medes and Persians, and had captured Ecbattana, their capital and residence … The said John advanced to the help of the Church of Jerusalem; but when her had reached the river [Tigris] he had not been able to take his army across the river in any vessel. He had then turned north, where he had learned that it was all frozen by the winter cold. He had lingered there for some time, waiting for the frost, but because of the wild weather … [was] forced to return home after losing much of his army because of the unaccustomed climate.*[117]

With a touch of color, the chronicler adds that Prester John is "said to be of the lineage of the Magi who are mentioned in the Gospel, and to rule over the same people as they did, enjoying such glory and prosperity that he is said to use only a sceptre of emerald."[117] If this reminds one of the emerald Grail, it is not surprising when we consider its bearer's lineage.

What was the truth behind this extraordinary account? At that time the threat of invasion from the East hung over the Western world rather like the threat of the atom bomb in the twentieth century. The perilously slender hold of the crusaders over the Kingdom of Jerusalem was constantly in danger of failing, with a consequent inrush of Muslim armies expected to follow. News of a crushing defeat "in the furthest East"

❡Lagran Magnificentia del Prete Ianni Signore dellindia Maggiore & della Ethiopia

Prester John, shown here on his throne, claimed to rule over an earthly paradise in the east.

was a morale booster comparable to hearing that the Russians had turned Hitler's forces back during World War II. Thus, there must have been a strong element of wish-fulfillment behind the various references to a "Christian king in the East."

Be that as it may, in 1165 a mysterious letter appeared, copies of which found their way to Pope Alexander III, the king of France, the emperor of Constantinople (Manuel Commenus), and the Holy Roman Emperor, Frederick II – the spiritual and temporal rulers of Western Christendom. The letter purported to come from no less a person than Prester John himself, and it is a most intriguing document. The letter begins:

Prester John, by the Grace of God most powerful king over all Christian kings, greetings to the Emperor of Rome and the King of France, our friends. We wish you to learn about us, our position, the government of our land, our people and our beasts ... And if you desire ... to come hither to our country, we shall make you on account of your good reputation our successors and we shall grant you vast lands, manors, and mansions.[117]

The letter continues in this style for some 20 pages, describing a land overflowing with goodness and riches, ruled over by the benign priest-king, whose crown is the "highest ... on earth" and whose sway extends over 42 other Christian kings. The writer then goes on to tell of the river Ydonis, which flows between his lands and those of the Saracens. The river flows out of the gates of paradise itself and is filled with precious stones. The letter ends by exhorting the rulers of Christendom to put to death "those treacherous Templars and pagans" and is signed "in the year five hundred and seven since our birth." The letter is a forgery, of this there can be no doubt. The style, as well as the contents, clearly derive from identifiable sources –

A sixteenth-century map places the realm of Prester John beyond Africa. Later traditions depicted this as the home of the Grail.

mostly Eastern – an ironic fact when we consider that Prester John was set up as a bitter foe of the Muslims! What we do have in the text of the letter is a description of the otherworld, a semi-attainable, paradisal place, filled with wonders and offering spiritual as well as temporal pleasures. We should hardly be surprised to find a Grail temple not unlike that described in *Der Jungere Titurel* to appear in this setting. Both are the product of the same impulse: the desire to return to the earthly paradise from which Adam and Eve were driven forth.

Prester John, whose title means "priest-king," is really the product of several vague historical personages, half-remembered accounts of Alexander the Great, various kings of Ethiopia, and more than one Tartar lord. In the letter, however, he is presented as something more than this: a spiritual king perceived as having withdrawn to an inner place, from where he watches over the progress of humanity and occasionally takes a direct hand in historical events. Merlin is another such, as are the biblical priests and prophets Melchizadek and Enoch, and King Arthur and Bran the Blessed.

Whether Wolfram found a reference to Prester John as the offspring of the Grail knight Lohengrin, or whether he made up the connection, he touched upon a deep nerve. John represented all that was best in Christendom. He suffered none of the traits of corruption or heresy that hung over much of the Western world like a dark cloud. He was all powerful, all good, and he was the guardian of a sacred land that housed many secrets – including the Grail.

From this point onward, the Grail seems to retreat further into inaccessible realms. Perhaps the destruction of the Templars and the connection of the Grail with the heretical Cathars made the subject too dangerous. Certainly within a few years of the fall of the Templars the spate of Grail literature slowed to a trickle, finally dying out altogether at the end of the fourteenth century. Later works, such as Thomas Malory's *Le Morte D'Arthur*, merely repeated or revised the older texts, adding little or nothing to the history of the sacred vessel.

But the story does not end here. Instead, the Grail performs another remarkable shift of shape and context – nevertheless maintained the same principles that had been part of its mythology from the beginning. It resurfaced next in the teachings of the most select and secretive groups in Europe. These hidden brotherhoods, whose members remained faithful to ancient beliefs and teachings and who sought the truth in more esoteric places than the mainstream, are the next focus of attention.

SECRET SOCIETIES

A stranger here
Strange Things doth meet
Strange Glories see.[122a]

THOMAS TRAHERNE POETICAL WORKS

At the end of the Arthurian era, the Grail seems to vanish from sight for a time. The Grail section of *Le Morte D'Arthur* appears final; a hand comes down from heaven, seizes the vessel, and carries it off, "after which let no man say that he has seen the Grail," says Malory. But the sacred vessel had not really gone at all – or at least not far. It simply took on new disguises, hiding itself among the hermetic notions of alchemy and the mysteries of a sect known as the Brotherhood of the Rose Cross or Rosicrucians.

The origins of alchemy go back so far into the mists of time that it is impossible to say when or even where it first appeared. Essentially, the alchemist is a child of the ancient smiths, whose ability to draw molten metal from the earth and create things from it made them seem godlike. From this beginning, alchemy developed into a complex system that hid its true purpose behind a screen of deliberately baffling symbolic language.

But the true nature of alchemy was not, as is often suggested, a form of primitive chemistry in which the

An alchemist contemplates the mystery of the philosopher's stone in this eighteenth-century picture.

alchemists sought to turn base metal into gold. They were far more interested in the creation of a mysterious substance, known as the *lapis philosophorum* or philosopher's stone, which they believed would give them power over life and death. The basic element of this they named the *prima material*, the "first material," which despite being composed of several bizarre substances, had more to do with the human spirit than with the earth.

HEAVENLY GOLD

Throughout the late Middle Ages and into the Renaissance the alchemists of Europe and the Middle East sought to transmute the human spirit into heavenly gold, to perfect all of creation, especially man. One of the greatest alchemists, Nicholas Flamel, writing around the middle of the fourteenth century, stated this clearly when he wrote: "Our work is the conversion and change of one being into another being, as from one thing into another thing, from debility to strength … from corporeality to spirituality."

This is very much a function of the Grail, which transforms those who go in search of it into spiritual beings, while the more ancient sacred vessels were the alembic in which the whole of creation was mixed, surely a most powerful image for alchemical work.

Alchemy has to do with "exchange" and "transformation," a mingling of the divine with the mundane. In the Grail legends there are constant veiled references to this. The very shape of the Grail as it was most commonly depicted – as a cup – illustrated this. The upper portion of the cup was a container for the spiritual essence that came from heaven, while the inverted cone of the base could be seen to represent humanity's reaching up toward perfection. The nexus point of the cup was where the substance of humanity encountered the essence of the divine and was transformed. Galahad, for instance, looked into the Grail and was changed.

The strange, rich symbolism of alchemy seems to have struck a deep chord in many people who sought to understand the mysteries of creation. The *lapis* itself was only a stage in the formation of a perfect human being, just as the Grail is but a symbol of the interior quest for spiritual perfection and oneness with God. Wolfram's *Parzival* is unique in describing the Grail as a stone, "of the purest kind"; the *lapsit exillis* which, it has been suggested, refers to the *lapis philosophorum* itself. Certainly the words he uses to describe this could come from any of the many treatises on alchemy:

A statue from the front of Chartres Cathedral shows the patriarch Melchizadek holding a Grail containing a stone.

They obtain life from a pure stone. Let me name it to you. It is called lapsit exillis. *The power of this stone enables the phoenix to burn itself to ashes and be reborn. The phoenix moults and changes its plumage, which is afterwards bright and shining and as glorious as ever. No human, however sick, would die for at least a week after he saw that stone. Nor would his looks fade. Indeed his appearance would be the same as on the day he saw the stone, as if he was in the very prime of life. If he could see the stone every day for two hundred years thereafter, his looks would never change, though his hair might turn grey. The name of the stone is the Grail.*[133]

By describing the Grail as a stone Wolfram brought it firmly into the realm of alchemy, where the quest for the elixir of life or for spiritual perfection, was ever after linked to the quest for the spiritual vessel. Just how deeply and profoundly this idea penetrated into the beliefs of the time can be seen from the fact that among the ornate allegorical statuary adorning the outside of Chartres Cathedral in France is the figure of the biblical priest-king Melchizadek. In his hands he holds a chalice in which a circular stone is set. The imagery combines seamlessly here. Melchizadek is seen as prefiguring Christ in offering bread and wine as a sacrament, the sacrament itself represents the communion of God and man, and the Grail he holds is a symbol of that divine feast. The stone represents the mysterious substance that extends life, the *lapis philosophorum*, or the *lapsit exillis*.

THE SACRED STONES

The search for the philosopher's stone hid an even deeper mystery – the quest for the origin of life itself – a search that was forbidden by every religious belief at the time. In the symbol-laden language of the alchemical writings we see the first speculations concerning the true nature of human procreation, heavily disguised in terms of a king and queen who represent the elements of flesh and spirit, entering a bath together, and there engendering the Mercurius, the spiritual child. An alchemist would have recognized the meaning of this at once – the bath is the alembic in which the elements are combined to produce the philosopher's stone.

Such ideas are even present in the more exoteric pages of the Grail literature. In that most mystical of texts, the thirteenth-century *Perlesvaus*, the Grail is said to undergo five changes of form "of which no one ought to speak."[13] The last of these changes is into the form of a child – a restatement of the divinity held by the vessel of the spirit and a clear reference to the Mercurius, the child born from the mingling of earth and spirit in the alchemist's alembic.

The fact that Wolfram's "pure stone" was also a stone fallen from heaven is of particular interest in the light of alchemical symbolism. In certain texts, the *lapis* was identified with the stone of Saturn. Saturn can be identified with Cronos, the god who, as we have already seen, is described as sleeping beneath the earth off the coast of Celtic Britain. According to the myth, Saturn vomited forth this stone after being tricked into swallowing it instead of his son, Zeus. The alchemists saw this as a symbol of the divine nature of the lapis, as something cast aside by the god. The stone of Saturn came to rest on Mount Helicon, the holy mountain of ancient Greece. It was thus a stone from heaven, which lay beyond the reach of all but a few, on top of a mountain rising from water – imagery strikingly similar to that of the Grail.

THE STONE OF MECCA

There is another stone that could have influenced Wolfram's conception of the Grail. This is the Black Stone, sacred to the Islamic religion, which stands at the center of Mecca, toward which the faithful offer daily prayers wherever they happen to be in the world. This stone is believed to have been a meteorite that fell out of the sky in the distant past; it was an object of worship until the time of the Prophet Muhammad, who denounced this and declared that it should instead be used as a means of communicating with God. According to the Koran, the Angel Gabriel gave the stone to the prophet Ishmael at the time of the rebuilding of the Kaaba, the Cubic House, where the stone still resides. In earlier times still, it was said to represent the triple-aspected Mother Goddess, the *Mater Dea*, who, with the god Hubal, were offered sacrifices of blood – a fact that becomes significant when it is considered in

This sixteenth-century Persian miniature shows the black meteoric stone of the Kaaba surrounded by worshippers.

connection with the Grail. Interestingly, the color green as related by Wolfram to the Grail stone, is associated with Venus, whose day, Friday, is the Islamic Sabbath; green is also the color associated with the Prophet and is therefore considered sacred in Islamic tradition.

The basis of the alchemical great work is a reconciliation of opposites, the creation of divine harmony in heaven and on earth, the practical and symbolic working out of the dictum "As above, so below," said to be inscribed on an emerald tablet and attributed to Hermes Trismagistus, the semidivine founder of alchemy. Perhaps because this tablet has been described as an emerald, as was the Grail, a further link was forged between the sacred vessel and the processes of alchemy.

Like the *lapis philosophorum* and the Black Stone, the Grail was an object of supernatural origin and activity, involving the prolonging of life, the birth of a divine child, the quest for wisdom and knowledge, and direct communion with God. That the image of the stone was capable of supporting such a wide range of interpretations is further demonstrated by the way it is used in biblical sources. For example, in the story of Jacob, who falls asleep with his head pillowed on a stone and dreams of a ladder leading directly to heaven, the meaning is clear, while in the Book of Revelation (2:17) it is written: "To him who conquers I will give some of the hidden manna, and I will give him a white stone with a new name written upon it." That new name is reserved for the individual who completes the great work or wins the Grail.

THE DIVINE VESSEL

All of this can be interpreted in mystical as well as in alchemical terms. In Catholic doctrine, the Virgin Mary is the vessel in which the divine child is brought to term. In alchemical symbolism, the Mercurius is manifested in the *vas mirabile* (miraculous vessel). Thus, the infinite is born into the finite, Christ becomes man, and spiritual transformations of the Grail and the alembic are shown to be the same. As the fourth-century theologian St. Ephraem wrote, invoking Christ:

In the womb that bore you are Fire and Spirit,
Fire and Spirit are in the river where you were baptized,
Fire and Spirit are in our baptism too,
And the Bread and Cup are Fire and Spirit.[11]

It is not surprising to find the troubadours, who fueled the Arthurian myths with their burning and joyful light, referring to Mary as "the Grail of the World" and applying the term with equal validity to the object of their human love:

The beloved one is the heart's Grail,
The lover will never be alone,
For to him she is the highest Grail,
Which protects him from every woe.

The child of Mercury is born inside an alchemical vessel in this seventeenth-century etching from the anonymous Book of Alchemy.

THE ROSICRUCIAN GRAIL

The centuries-long pursuit of the alchemical mysteries finally gave way to the dawn of science in the eighteenth century. The history of the mysterious Rosicrucian Brotherhood parallels this at several points. Both groups worked in the shadow of accusations of heresy from the Catholic Church, and both disguised their work in language of the cloudiest kind, where nothing was what it seemed.

The history of the Rosicrucians appears to have begun in the fourteenth century, but it was not for another 250 years that a document called *Fama Fraternitatis of the Meritorious Order of the Rose Cross* was published in Germany in 1641.[2] This work described the life and death of Christian Rosenkreutz, philosopher, mystic, and magician, who had apparently lived to 106 and whose body was then concealed in a secret tomb or vault, which remained undiscovered for another 120 years.

This would place Rosenkreutz at the end of the fourteenth or the beginning of the fifteenth century, though there are no records from that or indeed any time that relate to his actual existence. The description of the finding of the vault containing his uncorrupted remains is written in highly symbolic language, which reads like an initiatory text, and the opening of the vault is described as an event that could have far-reaching effects.

"When the vault is discovered, also there shall be opened a door to Europe which already hath begun to appear, and with great desire is expected of many."[2] One is reminded irresistibly of the forbidden door in the story of Bran the Blessed, though it is unlikely that this would still have been remembered in this time.

Judging by the reaction across Europe to the *Fama* and the manifestos that followed it, the desire and expectation must have been considerable. A new hope was seeded, which had nothing to do with the effects of the Renaissance, where medieval attitudes were still abroad and enlightenment battled uneasily with a mysticism that retained the blinkers of dogma and superstition.

No one knew the whereabouts of the Rosicrucian Brotherhood, but this did not stop many who read and understood the manifestos they produced from trying to make physical contact. The fact that there were writings that spoke of a brotherhood of adepts who could be contacted "through proper channels" was enough to prompt many to advertise in news-sheets for more information. Even the philosopher René Descartes went to Germany to seek out the brotherhood but, not surprisingly perhaps, found nothing. Yet on his return to Paris, he was forced to show himself publicly in order to prove that he had not become invisible – that he was not a Rosicrucian – for so had the rumors circulated.

When no reply was forthcoming to the various inquiries sent to nonexistent addresses or people, enthusiasts were driven to publish their own books and pamphlets to see whether their ideas resonated with other would-be Rosicrucians. Thus, the original manifestos spawned a succession of imitators and commentaries, constellating their writers into the formation of a mystery school whose doctrines were set out for all who could understand them to read – an odd reversal of the classical schools, which hid their teachings from all but their initiates.

The language employed in the Rosicrucian documents is allusive and full of symbolism, which must have prevented all but those in the know from understanding what was being said. In reality, most of what they had to say was couched in a combination of esoteric Christianity and ancient mystery-school teaching that had been kept alive by the alchemists. Rosicrucianism itself survived because it had no visible foundation, no headquarters, no officers, no dogmas, and no rules of membership. The effect of this on the European world of the seventeenth century was deep and lasting, paving the way for the great esoteric revivals of the eighteenth and nineteenth centuries. It also brought a new dimension into the history of the Grail, drawing on the oldest levels of the myth as well as on some of the primary themes that had gathered around it in the medieval period.

In the symbolically charged literature of the Rosicrucians we see an unfolding of the original Grail story in a new form. Here, as so often in the past, an outwardly rigid spirituality is underpinned by an esoteric core. The Rosicrucian movement has just such an esoteric resonance, flowering within the strict confines of Protestantism, just as the Grail myths flowered within the outwardly immovable tenets of Catholicism.

Much of this occurred at a time when the medieval world was beginning to give way before the approach of the Renaissance, when knowledge, both accepted and forbidden, drew upon the mysteries of the past and, only half understanding them, recast them in a form that better fitted the time. All of this comes together in a cluster of symbolism surrounding the images of the vessel itself and takes us back into the strange image-laden texts of the alchemists who hid their deepest mysteries in language that spoke of one thing when it meant another.

THE WEDDING

The central text of the Rosicrucian mysteries is called "The Chymical Wedding of Christian Rosecross," a mystical sequence that celebrates the mystical wedding of Christian Rosenkreutz and the Lady Venus, disguised as the symbolic marriage of a king and queen. Written in allusive language, it is full of hints and clues that are almost never followed up.

Christian Rosenkreutz himself is encountered first. Although his hair is grey and he accounts himself no longer young, he shares the same innocent earnestness as Perceval in the Grail myths at the outset of the quest. Here is one who would sell all that he has for the possession of the pearl of wisdom and who suffers the rigors of his initiation into wisdom with the greatest humility and determination. His approach is ideal for a candidate toward initiation, unaware that although he has been invited to a royal wedding, he himself is the groom. In the same way, Perceval sets out to find the Grail and is at once the guest in the castle where it is hidden, though he does not know this, and begins a quest that will take him full circle, back to this point of beginning.

Christian Rosenkreutz and Perceval both suffer the lot of all men. They are thrust into incarnation, where they are yoked to their fellows by the service they both offer to the quest. We see this in the "Chymical Wedding," in which Christian dreams that he emerges from the dungeon into which he has been placed with the help of "an ancient matron." As he does so, he is wounded and is covered in blood from head to foot. His rescuer tells him that he should be proud of his wounds and "keep them for my sake." There are echoes here of the Christ-like Perceval and of the wounded Fisher King of the Grail.

Christian arrays himself for the wedding with crossed red bands over his breast and four red roses in his hat. These roses proclaim his loyalty to the goddess and show that for all its Protestant veneer the "Chymical Wedding" is in fact an exposition of the mysteries of Venus, which can be traced back to the practices of pagan Europe and to the Grail myth itself in the parallels between the Venusburg of German folklore and the holy mountain of Rosicrucian and Grail myths. The roses are an indication of the initiate's dedication to his task:

The disciple, servant of the Rose and of the Cross, progressing along the narrow Path and passing through the narrow gateway of Initiation, keeps ever before his eyes the Goal, remote at first, but ever growing nearer. From the beginning he has been pledged to the finding of Unity, for Unity stands at the end of the Path.[10]

That path leads, inevitably, upward to the Mountain of Salvation, the site of the Grail temple where the mysteries of unity with the infinite are celebrated.

THE MOUNTAIN OF THE GRAIL

The way to the Grail is not easy, for it is mountainous and guarded by wild animals and powerful otherworldly opponents. In the Grail myths this includes challenging figures, such as the hideous Grail messenger, sometimes called Kundry, who urges the Grail knights on their way when they are beginning to fall by the wayside, often with cruel and hurtful gibes. However, it is the mountain that remains the most fearsome and terrible trial.

In Rosicrucian terms, this is perfectly described in an allegory known as *The Holy Mountain*, attributed to the seventeenth-century alchemist Thomas Vaughan. The following description is given:

A seventeenth-century illustration from a collection of Rosicrucian emblems depicts the mysterious mountain of the philosophers.

> *There is a mountain situated in the midst of the earth or centre of the world, which is both small and great. It it soft, yet also above measure hard and stony. It is far off and near at hand, but by the providence of God, invisible. In it are hidden the most ample treasures, which the world is not able to value. This mountain ... is compassed about with very cruel beasts and ravening birds – which make the way thither both difficult and dangerous.*[2]

If the seeker succeeds in daring all these perils, in recognizing that the mountain is not just a mountain and the treasure not just a treasure, he will find:

> *The most important thing [on the mountain] and the most powerful, is a certain exalted Tincture, with which the world ... might be touched and turned into most pure gold. This Tincture ... will make you young when you are old, and you will perceive no disease in any part of your bodies.*[2]

This is so like the function of the Grail as described by Wolfram that it is hard not to believe that its author was directly influenced by the medieval texts, though it is more likely that both are an expression of a hunger for spiritual enlightenment. But there is yet another parallel between the story told by Wolfram and one of the most fundamental aspects of the Rosicrucian movement. In *Parzival* we read:

> *Those who are appointed to be the guardians of the Grail are thus identified. On the surface of the Stone an inscription appears which announces the name and lineage of the one who is called upon to make a journey into the world … Happy is the mother of any child destined to serve in this place! Rich and poor alike rejoice if a child of theirs is called to the Company of the Grail! They come from many countries and they are ever after immune from shame and look forward to a rich reward in Heaven.*[133]

This mirrors ideas described in the Rosicrucian text *Fama Fraternitatis* of the existence of a brotherhood selected and called by God to bear witness to the great mystery of Christian Rosenkreutz, and whose task is to remain hidden until the time when the world is ready for their message. Another great alchemist, Robert Fludd, in a defense of the Rosicrucian Brotherhood, makes the connection even clearer when he says:

> *Here then you have [a] House … of Wisdom erected on the Mount of Reason. It remains, however, to learn who are those … to whom this House is open. These most fortunate of men are described by the Apostle in the following manner: [as those who] come, as unto as living stone … who build up a spiritual house … A chosen generation, a royal priesthood, an holy community, a ransomed people, [who] should practice the virtues of Him who has called you out of darkness into his royal light. For previously you were not a people, but now you are the people of God.*[2]

This is certainly an echo of the "Christian progeny bred to a pure life [who] have the duty of keeping [the Grail]" in Wolfram's poem. Both are summoned to their task in the same way as were the Arthurian knights who set out on the quest for the Grail. Both are at the center of a search for spiritual reality that transcends the mundane world of everyday.

THE CASTLE OF THE GRAIL

Those who succeed in climbing the Mountain of Salvation, who brave the wild beasts and survive the terrors of the journey, find themselves at last at the castle or temple where the Grail is kept.

As we have seen, this has its own specific location. But it is clear that more than one actual place – the Takht-i-Taqdis in particular – bears an uncanny resemblance to the description of the Grail temple in *Der Jungere Titurel*. But this is not the only site modelled on the home of the sacred vessel. One such place is Castle Karlstein in the present-day Czech Republic. Its deliberate design brings together the story of the Grail with the mysterious history of the Rosicrucian Brotherhood. The Bohemian king, Charles IV, built Karlstein between 1348 and 1365, soon after the first flowering of Grail literature. Described as "the last initiate on the throne of the Emperors,"[2] Charles understood the connection between the Rosicrucian mysteries and those of the Grail perhaps better than anyone in his time. Karlstein was built to reflect this, as the following description shows:

The Golden Chapel in Castle Karlstein (Bohemia). Built at the behest of King Charles IV, this castle also contained a room intended to represent the Chapel of the Grail.

The adornment of the walls in the various chapels to be found in the castle, with their quantities of semi-precious stones and gold, the way in which the light is diffused through these semi-precious stones which – set in gilded lead – take the place of window glass, lead one to conclude that Charles IV knew about the powers of precious stones and gold. The small chapel of St Catherine, for example, is a veritable gem. The entire walls, up to the ceiling, are inlaid with semi-precious stones such as amethyst, jasper, cornelian and agate, while the cross vaulting above has a blue background, adorned with roses, according to the Rosicrucian motif. According to tradition it was here that Charles IV withdrew every year from Good Friday to Easter Sunday in order to meditate in undisturbed privacy.[2]

Easter is not only associated with the Crucifixion and Resurrection of Christ, but also with the Grail mysteries, which take place at this time. The design of the castle reflects this in a number of ways. Throughout the building are murals that refer to the initiation of Christian Rosenkreutz – the releasing of the prisoner from his chains, the sowing of seed in darkness, its milling and baking. All of these are also aspects of the alchemical process as described in countless documents from the Middle Ages onward: the burial of the dead, the feast that reminds us of the wedding banquet in the "Chymical Wedding," and finally, execution and dismemberment.

These images guide the seeker toward the great tower of the castle, which is approached across a narrow bridge, echoing the Sword Bridge of the Grail story. Within the tower is the Chapel of the Holy Cross, again decorated with semiprecious stones, beneath a roof representing the sun, moon, and stars, interspersed with a motif of roses. The windows are formed of pure topaz, amethyst, and almandine, through which the light enters in bands of glorious color. The symbolism is clear: he who follows the path of the initiate, who seeks the Grail, makes his way through life, learning, forgetting, relearning, following the processes of spiritual alchemy until he is able to cross the perilous bridge and enter the chamber of the mysteries. The parallels need hardly be spelled out. This is the chapel of the Grail and of the rose.

Here, indeed, the symbolism of the Grail and the rose come together. To seek one is to seek the other. To follow one form of enlightenment is to find another. The rose blossoms within and from the Grail; Rosicrucianism stems from the root of the Grail myths as a natural outgrowth of the spiritual search.

The alchemist Arnold of Vilanova said: "Make a round circle and you have the philosopher's stone." The Grail, whether as a stone, a cup, a container, or that which is contained, remains at the center of the circle. But the center is also the circumference, and all quests lead to this place. The knights in their wanderings, like the disciples of Christian Rosenkreutz, attain the goal that would have remained inaccessible had they gone purposely to the Grail castle by a direct route. In surrendering themselves to chance, they are enabled to make the way to the heart of the mystery, where some will pluck the rose or drink from the cup of truth.

THE OCCULT REVIVAL

In the years following the activity of the Rosicrucian Brotherhood, the appreciation of the Grail became more and more esoteric. It now began to have more to do with the work of ceremonial magicians who internalized the quest for the Grail, making it an interior journey.

The eighteenth century witnessed the discarding of many ancient beliefs and traditions, such as those of Gnosticism and alchemy, which were no longer considered to have any value. But the pendulum swung the other way during the next century. At this time various occult groups were set up with the declared intention of studying and practicing the mysteries, as they had been defined thousands of years before. This movement became known as the occult revival, and a number of men and women, among them Madame Helena Blavatsky, Aleister Crowley, and A. E. Waite, achieved notoriety as practitioners of the magical arts.

Madame Blavatsky and Colonel Henry Steel Olcott, pictured here, were in the forefront of the occult revival during the nineteenth and early twentieth centuries.

The Grail became an essential part of such magical work. From the moment Robert de Borron wrote of how Christ spoke to Joseph of Arimathea "holy words that are sweet and gracious ... called the secrets of the Grail,"[14] he assured that seekers would appear who would desire to know those secrets. The nineteenth and twentieth centuries saw an increasing number of such seekers, each one determined to experience the power of the Grail.

Much of the fascination with the Grail in esoteric circles focused around the revisiting of older traditions. In our own time, there are new Templar organizations and even modern followers of the Cathars, who have looked back to the Middle Ages in order to find a new understanding of the Grail. One such contemporary organization, a modern Templar Order, states in its literature that:

> *It is a fundamental belief of the Templar tradition, a belief backed by long experience, that if the seeker after truth begins to work seriously on himself, he will start to radiate light on the inner levels ... Every man and woman who is stirred by stories, legends, or films of noble heroes is really reacting to the promptings of the True Knight who sleeps within the heart ... [and] which will guide us inevitably to the Grail.*[30]

The Order of the Golden Dawn brought together a number of spiritual sources, including those of the Grail.

Modern Cathar movements have also made an appearance in recent times and declared themselves to be founded firmly on Grail spirituality. In particular, the Lectorium Rosicrucianum, founded by J. van Rijckenborgh and Catharose di Petrie in 1952, has continued to grow and disseminate ideas that combine elements of Cathar beliefs with those of the Rosicrucian Brotherhood. A guiding light in the order's early days was Antonine Gadal, who later changed his name to Galaad, after the greatest of the Grail knights, and founded a center in the Pyrenees (also called Galaad), which was devoted to the restoration of Cathar ideals and to the discovery of the Grail itself.

One of Gadal's associates for a time was the Irish writer Francis Rolt-Wheeler, who later made his own contribution to Grail literature in his book *Mystic Gleams from the Holy Grail*, in which he gave an account of the stories from a generally esoteric viewpoint:

> *The legend of the Holy Grail glows ... with an inner light of esoterism [sic]. Few indeed be those who have sought to follow the silver thread of spiritual Initiation in this strange and mysterious cycle of Miracle, of Faery, of Chivalry,*

and of a Super-sacrament. Consequently, in this mystical legend, there is a glimpse of the unknown; the reader may lose his way inside the visions.[112]

Despite Francis Rolt-Wheeler's rather colorful style, there is much in his book that depicts the depths of understanding of the Grail's inner mysteries among modern esotericists.

Inevitably, the Rosicrucian movement has also had its modern devotees. More than one writer has seen it as the natural inheritor of the Grail tradition. In particular, Manley Palmer Hall, who founded the Philosophical Research Society in the United States in 1936, linked Templars, Cathars, and Rosicrucians with the Grail, stating that "it is evident that the story of ... the symbolic genealogy of the Grail kings relates to the descent of schools or orders of initiates."[54]

One of the most prestigious esoteric groups, the Hermetic Order of the Golden Dawn, began working with Arthurian architects as long ago as 1896, and after this several offshoots, including the Society of Inner Light, the Stella Matutina, and the Servants of the Light, have all drawn upon the esoteric elements within the Grail story to form working magical groups.

One of the founding members of the Golden Dawn, A. E. Waite, postulated a secret church of the Grail in his 1930 volume *The Holy Grail: Its Legends and Symbolism.* He suggests the presence of a mystical body of thought, almost without form, but threading its way throughout the entire literature of the Grail.

The presence of this ... secret church is like that of [unseen] angels. In the outer courts are those who are prepared for regeneration and in the adytum there are those who never attained it: these are the Holy Assembly. It is the place of those who, after the birth of flesh, which is the birth of the will of man, have come to be born of God ... It is the place of the waters of life, with the power to drink freely. It is like the still, small voice: it is heard only in the midst of the heart's silence, and there is no written word to tell us how its rite is celebrated, but it is like a priesthood within the priesthood ... There are no admissions – at least of the ceremonial kind – to the Holy Assembly; it is as if in the last resort a candidate inducts himself. There is no sodality, no institution, no order ... it is not a revelation so much as an inheritance ... It is the place of those to have become transmuted.[124]

Despite Waite's words, many groups and individuals have continued to assume the existence of such a secret church, or in some instances set themselves the task of founding it. The Anthroposophical Society, founded by Rudolf Steiner in 1913 as a breakaway from the earlier Theosophists, has had the Grail at its heart from the beginning. Steiner himself wrote a considerable amount on the subject, including this prophetic passage from his *Occult Science: An Outline*:

> *The Hidden Knowledge flows, although quite unnoticed at the beginning, into the mode of thinking of the men of this period ... the hidden knowledge which from this side takes hold of mankind now and will take on more and more in the future, may be called symbolically the wisdom of the Grail. The modern initiates may, therefore, also be called initiates of the Grail.*[120]

More recently, the Servants of the Light, which describes itself as a school of esoteric science, has made use of specifically Arthurian and Grail materials as the foundation of its inner work. Some privately issued papers give an idea of the material involved: *Grail Centres, Alexandria, Gnostics and the Grail* are anonymous works, while *The Grail Lectures* of S. F. Annet[4] include "The Grail Tests" and "The Gnostic Hypostases and the Grail Legend." The former examines the initiation of Arthurian knighthood with emphasis on the chivalry of the Grail, which the writer finds to embody the concept of inner strength and "self-reverence, self-knowledge, self-control," which "alone raise man to sovereign power."[4]

Other esoteric groups have continued to work with the Grail into our own time. The Aurum Solis or the Order of the Sacred Word, originally founded by Charles Kingold and George Stanton in 1897, and more recently continued by Melita Denning and Osborne Phillips, has released some of the order's secret papers in the form of a series of books published under the general title of *The Magical Philosophy*. Within are numerous references to the Grail, which permeates the ceremonies and teaching of the order.

In the United States, the San Grail Sodality, founded by the British esotericist William G. Gray in the 1980s, is based on a study of the Qabala and the Western mystery tradition and includes a series of ceremonies and sacraments loosely based on the Grail mysteries as part of its practical work. This is a prime example of a modern mystery school founded on the principles of the Grail. During the 1980s, the respected ceremonial magician Gareth Knight led a number of workshops that brought into being a company very like that described by Waite, having no constitution, no sodality, and no initiation beyond that of a simple presence and participation in the work. A ritual Catechism of the Grail, first performed in 1981, is still in regular use among those present at these latter-day Arthurian mysteries.[97]

All of those who have sought the sacred vessel by whatever means shared the desire to bring the world of the "great above" into conjunction with the world below. This theme has been part of the Grail story from the start and remains just as potent and essential to those who seek the Grail through the restoration of ancient esoteric rites.

This gives some idea of the richness of a tradition still in operation, which draws upon the Grail stream for its inspiration and energy. The writer Charles Williams, who was a member of the Golden Dawn, described how a modern order of the Grail might appear. This is closer to Waite's idea of a mystical brotherhood than a proper magical order. Williams wrote about it in the end of his study of the Holy Spirit in the following terms:

A. E. Waite wrote extensively on the secret history of the Grail, dealing with its magical traditions.

The apprehension of this order, in nature and in grace, without and within Christendom, should be, now, one of our chief concerns ... [It] would have no easy labour. But, more than can be imagined, it might find that in this present world, its labour was never more needed, its concentration never more important, its profits never perhaps more great.[128]

This speaks of the need for the Grail to be still at work in the world. That it is so seems apparent, for despite the dark times in which we live, there are still gleams of light that betray the presence of the Grail. Some of these mystic gleams have found their way into the contemporary world through movies, fiction, and an endless fascination with the continuing mystery of the Grail.

A NEW KNIGHTHOOD
OF THE GRAIL

Let not him who seeks cease until he finds,
and when he finds he shall be astonished.[107]

The Gospel of Thomas. Trans. Gilles Quispel

Only recently has it become possible to view the story of the Grail as something like a connected history. Before that it existed simply as a set of moments, peaks in the beliefs and traditions of our world. Now that we have access to so many sources of spiritual process, we can see that the sacred vessel has been present from the beginning of history. Like Sophia or the Shekinah, the Grail came into exile from paradise with humankind, and, despite all the different ways we have chosen to understand it, it has

The quest for the Grail was very much a search for the lost paradise from which mankind is exiled. (Detail from The Earthly Paradise *by Brueghel.)*

remained an unwavering presence ever since, leading us to discover new depths of understanding and truth about ourselves and our relationship with the infinite.

This is what makes the Grail such an enduring symbol, one that each age has recognized since its first appearance in the world. People have been seeking to fathom the mystery of the Grail ever since, with varying degrees of success. It remains a living symbol and the object of a continuing quest. Those who seek the Grail today –whether scholars or mystics – constitute a new kind of knighthood as true to the original precepts of chivalry, honor, and truth as were the Knights of the Round Table.

Within the stories of the Grail, seekers have found extraordinary clues to contemporary living and a profound source of individual healing. The story of the Wounded King contains parallels with almost every level of life as we know it today. We are all, in essence, wounded, and to experience the restoring of the king can bring personal healing in its wake. Beyond this, the Grail represents not only our origins, but also the divine spark that we cannot help but perceive within our humanity.

THE PSYCHOLOGY OF MYTH

These ideas are part of the modern discipline of psychoanalysis that has borrowed heavily from the Grail myth; in so doing, it has learned a great deal about the human condition and also explored the Grail story in great depth. Nor is this surprising, considering how much evidence there is for the antiquity and depth of the sacred vessel's presence in history.

Inevitably, in the light of the Grail's extreme potency as a symbol, the leading psychologist and exponent of symbolism regarded it very seriously. Carl Gustav Jung (1875–1961), whose exploration of the human psyche transformed the approach to psychoanalysis, encountered the Grail early in his life. Thereafter, it cast a powerful spell over him and featured extensively in his work and in his personal life.

Jung, along with Sigmund Freud, changed the direction of thinking in psychoanalysis in the last years of the nineteenth century. But Jung's approach was very different from that of his former colleague Freud; Jung recognized the importance of the inner spiritual truths present within the unconscious mind. Since then, a revolution in personal therapies, self-help, and the inner search has grown and multiplied until there are countless ways to discover the deep mythical call within the individual. Many of these ways have drawn, either consciously or unconsciously, on the work of the great Swiss analyst, whose writings continued to inspire and challenge those who are involved in the inner quest.

The Grail legends were of considerable importance to Jung, although it was left to his wife Emma to publish the results of her own considerable researches into their meaning after his death. The matter of the quest influenced Jung's work throughout his life, and the legends themselves illuminated significant stages in his own development as well as his thinking.

In his thirties, as Jung was beginning to make a name for himself, he dreamed that he met, in the middle of a busy modern city, a knight in armor with a red cross emblazoned on his breast. At once Jung knew that this was the Grail knight and that he had come to point Jung toward the importance of this myth. In his autobiography, Jung adds:

The great Swiss psychoanalyst C. G. Jung was fascinated by the Grail, which he saw as a symbol of transformation.

I had an inkling that a great secret lie hidden in these stories [of the Grail]. Therefore it seemed quite natural to me that the dream should conjure up the world of the knights of the Grail ... or that was in the deepest sense, my world.[59]

From this point on Jung felt himself to be on a personal quest for the Grail. Shortly after this important dream he broke away from mainstream psychoanalytical work and from his partnership with Freud, deciding instead to follow his own course, one that led him into the world of the spirit and universal consciousness. The process he discovered, which he termed "individuation," reflected the journey of Perceval in search of the sacred vessel as it was present in everyone.

For Jung, this was an inward journey to the center of being, which he called the Self. In that center, the individual could encounter a divine presence, an inner sense of identity that transcended the outward shape of the egocentric personality. The mirror of the Grail experience was precisely this, and Jung knew it.

A study of the Grail myths led Jung into the region of alchemy, where he found the intricate and mysterious language of the adepts perfectly suited to the interpretation of his patients' dream states and neuroses. Like the medieval writers and proto-scientists before him, he saw how deeply the Grail myth was embedded in the human spirit from cradle to grave. Much later in his life, he had another major dream in which he visited the castle of the Grail, but could not enter it. He found himself in a bare, rocky landscape that resembled the Wasteland of the Grail myth. As the dream ended, he arrived at a lake with an island on which stood the Grail castle. He was preparing to swim out to the castle as he awoke. He had visited the gates of the otherworld.

The image of the Grail continued to haunt Jung to the end of his life. In the gardens of the center he created at Dornach in Switzerland stands a small, carved stone dedicated to the *genius loci*, the invisible spirit of place. On its side is carved an image of the Grail. Jung knew that it represented the unseen meeting point of the human and the divine.

JACQUES DE MOLAY, chef des Templiers
(XIIIe siècle)

Jacques de Molay, last grand master of the Templars. Jung dreamed of meeting a red cross knight and saw this as a pointer to the mysteries of the Grail.

JOSEPH CAMPBELL AND THE GRAIL

Jung's work paved the way for a fresh examination of myth. Students and followers of his methods such as Alfred Adler (1870–1937) and Marie-Louise von Franz (1915–98) extended the work Jung had begun, often referring to the Grail.[58]

American mythographer Joseph Campbell (1904–87) wove myth into the modern world by showing that it possessed important messages for everyone. In seminal works such as *The Hero with a Thousand Faces*, *The Masks of God*, and the best-selling *The Power of Myth* he produced the most powerful set of interpretations of myth in our time. *The Power of Myth* was based on the hugely successful TV series of the same name, which had audiences glued to their TV sets over the six weeks of its screening in 1987. Campbell's work awakened a latent fascination for myth that has been present in mankind from the earliest times, making it respectable and fascinating for a whole new generation.

Joseph Campbell, arguably the finest mythographer of our time, saw great relevance in the stories of the Grail.

Throughout his life Campbell followed his own myth with as much determination as the Grail knights followed their obsession with the sacred vessel, describing this memorably as "following your bliss," a term that quickly became enshrined in contemporary thinking. His influence has reached further, even into Hollywood, where George Lucas drew heavily on *The Hero with a Thousand Faces* when writing and filming the first *Star Wars* trilogy.

For Campbell, the Grail myth represented a deep sense of yearning for something unknown, but not unknowable. He knew that all seekers, even when they had little or no idea what they were looking for, or how to find it, sensed that whatever was there to be discovered must lie within the individual. Campbell's views were very like Jung's: both saw the idea of individuation, the discovery of the personal vision, as central to human development; both recognized in the stories of the Grail a perfect symbol of this search. Campbell saw myth as central to the development of the human imagination. Nowhere has he said this more clearly than in the following words:

Throughout the inhabited world, in all times and under every circumstance, the myths of man have flourished, and they have been a living inspiration of whatever else may have appeared out of the activities of the human body and mind. It would not be too much to say that myth is the secret opening through which the inexhaustible energies of the cosmos pour into human cultural manifestations.[16]

This applies so exactly to the mystery of the Grail that it could hardly be better said. Campbell's understanding of the essential meaning of the Grail transcended the need to look for physical manifestations. "Cultural manifestations" are and were a different matter. The Grail has always been indissolubly tied to the developments of human culture. Its mystery is central to our understanding and relationship with deity, with the infinite, and with the source of all spiritual enlightenment.

NEW VISIONS

There can be, in the final analysis, no end to the stories of the Grail. Even if it was to be somehow proved beyond doubt that the sacred vessel had been found, or that it could be codified and quantified, stories about it would continue to circulate.

Contemporary treatments of the Grail story, both in fiction and nonfiction, have abounded throughout the last century and have brought a whole new spectrum of meaning and relevance to the Grail in our time. A vast number of books has appeared, many dealing with the Grail from new directions. Since there are far too many of these to deal with adequately here, we shall concentrate on a handful that push the mystery of the Grail to new levels of awareness in contemporary terms.

Surprisingly, perhaps, the Grail has not featured overly in the history of cinema. Other than a brief appearance in the hugely popular film *Indiana Jones and the Last Crusade*, directed by Steven Spielberg and written by George Lucas, it has been largely ignored. Two exceptions are John Boorman's masterpiece *Excalibur* (1981), which to date is the only film to integrate the Grail into the Arthurian mythos as closely as it was in the Middle Ages; and Terry Gilliam's extraordinary modern Grail fable *The Fisher King*, which appeared in 1991.

Perceval le Gallois, written and directed by Eric Rohmer and based on Chrétien de Troyes's work, is another attempt to capture the Grail story on film, perhaps the finest yet. Released in 1978, it offered a unique approach in that Rohmer rejects the usual trappings of Hollywood and

The archetypal treasure hunter, Indiana Jones (Harrison Ford) sought the Grail in the 1989 film Indiana Jones and the Last Crusade.

attempts to portray the Middle Ages with highly stylized sets. This is about as near as we can get to what a medieval filmmaker might have produced, had cinematography been discovered several hundred years earlier than it actually was.

The result is a quirky masterpiece that retells the tale of the innocent Perceval and the equally naive Gawain in the quest for the Grail. Rohmer adapts the original poem by Chrétien de Troyes, using his own translation of the text and following it almost word for word. Perceval proceeds from one encounter to another, stealing a kiss from a distressed damsel,

Eric Rohmer's 1978 film Perceval le Gallois, *follows the story of Chrétien de Troyes faithfully, setting it in a stylized landscape.*

falling in love, killing his enemies, visiting King Arthur's court, and becoming a knight. Rohmer observes this educational odyssey with an ironic wit that is reminiscent of his contemporary comedies.

This is neither a realistic nor a modern interpretation. The actors speak in rhyming couplets, and a chorus playing medieval instruments provides much of the narrative. The sets are symbolic, with sculpted metal trees, cardboard castles, and painted skies reflecting the stylistic nature of the paintings and illuminations from the original manuscript.

Rohmer, however, departs from Chrétien's unfinished text by omitting the final adventures of Gawain in order to focus on those of Perceval alone. At the point where Chrétien's narrative breaks off, with a comment that Perceval simply learned the meaning of Good Friday, Rohmer takes the bold step of adding his own ending to the story by having Perceval take the central role in an enactment of a medieval passion play. The hero's spiritual rebirth is thus shown as a union with Christ.

NEW STORIES OF THE GRAIL

Among the vast outpouring of Arthurian fiction and poetry written over the past thirty years, fewer have attempted to enter the territory of the Grail. Those who have done so tend to be writers of science fiction, whose utopian visions make an ideal resting place for the Grail of the future. Looking at these, one sees how the presence of the sacred vessel in our consciousness might continue to grow.

One contemporary writer who explored the myths of the Grail at a profound level is Charles Williams (1886–1945). His two volumes of poems, *Taliesin Through Logres* and *The Region of the Summer Stars* offer some of the most enlightening interpretations of the subject ever written. He also dealt with the Grail in the modern world in a novel *War in Heaven*. Here the Grail is an archetypal object found within the world; the book deals with the struggle for its possession by the forces of good and evil. The book begins memorably: "The telephone bell was ringing wildly but without result, since there was no one in the room but the corpse." This is the beginning of a fantastic modern quest, undertaken by a publisher's clerk, an archdeacon of the Anglican Church and a member of the peerage, who each in his own way correspond to the three most famous Grail knights: Galahad, Perceval, and Bors.

Ranged against this unlikely trio are three servants of the negative side of creation led by Gregory Persimmons, a long-time practitioner of small evils. He walks the left-hand path of magic and is determined to become one with the evil god he worships. He is the murderer of the man found in the room at the beginning of the book, and he desires the Grail to use a talisman of power to bind the soul of a child to his own perverted ends.

After the discovery of the corpse, the police declare themselves baffled. But stranger things are afoot. By chance we discover that the Grail is kept in the archdeacon's own church, and though he attaches little importance to it, he decides it must not fall into the hands of the evildoers who would misuse its power for their own ends. The rest of the book is taken up with an exciting chase across the English countryside, with the archdeacon and his two friends carrying the Grail to safety. A powerful ally helps them in the person of Prester John who, in Williams's book, is the guardian of the Grail for our own time. After some breathtaking magical battles, the enemies of the Grail are defeated, and the climax of the book sees the archdeacon celebrating mass with the cup – a modern Grail mass that reflects every other use to which the vessel has been put. This is, as the archdeacon realizes, an object that has been closer to Christ than any other thing surviving in the world. It becomes more than a relic; rather it is a doorway between the worlds, a point of contact between God and man. The essence of the Grail thus remains the same as it has always been in this fictional interpretation, which draws on its author's knowledge of medieval spirituality to make a powerful and moving statement.

Michael Moorcock, one of the finest contemporary myth-makers, has drawn much of his inspiration from the mythos of Arthur. Graf Ulrich von Beck, the hero of *The War-Hound and the World's Pain*, is a brutal soldier of fortune hardly in the Arthurian mold, yet he is singled out by no less than Lucifer to go in quest of a cure for the world's pain – which is, not surprisingly, the Grail. Lucifer's desire is to be reconciled with heaven and perhaps to take up his former position, but not all of hell's denizens share this wish. Before Beck's quest is over he must face the legions of the damned. Beck does find the Grail and gives it to Lucifer, but it is insufficient to heal the breach between heaven and hell – Lucifer is still not welcome in heaven. Instead he is given the task of redeeming earth and of learning the true nature of the Grail. When both the Devil and mankind can do this, all shall be redeemed. But there is a warning. Lucifer declares:

> *You are your own masters. Your lives are your own. Do you not see that this means an end to the miraculous? You are at the beginning of a new age for Man, an age of investigation and analysis.*[100]

Where this "age of investigation and analysis" leads we well know; the hope is that a rediscovery of the miraculous will follow. If the trend in science fiction writing and current scientific thought is any indication, this may well be so.

THE RETURN OF THE GRAIL

An age-old theme is the one that brings Arthur out of otherworldly retirement when the world needs him, and this has been explored in several recent novels that also deal with the Grail. These are *The Drawing of the Dark* by Tim Powers and *A Midsummer Tempest* by Poul Anderson.

In Tim Powers's book the Western world of the sixteenth century is threatened by the power of Sulieman's Ottoman Empire. Europe will fall unless the Fisher King, the Soul of the Land, is revived and brought to the field of battle. This can be brought about only by thwarting a plot to prevent the ancient monarch from drinking a special brew of beer, known as Hartzwesten Dark (the dark heart of the West?). The only person who can prevent this is Arthur, and he is long dead. But is he? In Powers's version of history, Merlin, who is still active at this late time, discovers that Arthur's soul has been reborn in the body of an Irish mercenary soldier named Brian Duffy. With the help of Excalibur he succeeds in reawakening Arthur's memories in time to avert disaster. The only problem is that when Arthur remembers everything, including his death at Camlann, he will once again withdraw.

In *A Midsummer Tempest* the Arthurian theme is subliminal, but nonetheless important. A parallel timeline is created in this novel in which the Industrial Revolution has happened in the time of King Charles I and Cromwell, with the Royalist cavaliers standing against, and the Roundheads for, the progress of the mechanical over the natural. Prince Rupert of the Rhine, accompanied by faithful friends, invokes the aid of the Faery King Oberon and Queen Titania in a quest for the staff and book of Prospero. (In this world the works of William Shakespeare, "the Great Historian," are represented as fact.) After many adventures, the staff and book are found, and a final confrontation takes place on Glastonbury Tor. Rupert invokes and succeeds in raising the Spirit of the Land, something older and more basic than the mere heroes of the past. Arthur and the knights of Avalon ride forth against the

Glastonbury Tor has long been described as a hiding place for the Grail.

armies of Cromwell, the representatives of the brick and mortar, and wheels and cogs of mechanistic rule. There are echoes here of Tolkien's *The Lord of the Rings* trilogy and the march of the Ents against Isengard. Here also science fiction seems to laugh at itself, taking the side of magic over science.

Those works in which the Grail appears produce a synthesis of the ageless myth represented by the Arthurian ethos, and what might legitimately be called the new mythology of science fiction. Sometimes, as in Roger Zelazny's story *The Last Defender of Camelot*, the mystery will almost be explained away, only to be replaced by another greater one, which – thank heaven – no one has yet succeeded in explaining. Or, as in works like Walter M. Miller's classic, *A Canticle for Leibowitz* it looms central to the matter of the story.

In Miller's book monks, hermits, and pseudosaints occupy a post-holocaust wasteland where the Grail makes a fleeting but important appearance. Toward the end of the story, one of the characters, significantly called Mrs. Grales, is making her confession to a latter-day priest of this future earth. But Mrs. Grales has two heads,

One of the finest modern retellings of the Grail myths is Corbenic *by Catherine Fisher, for which this atmospheric cover sets the scene.*

one purely vestigial, a supernumerary growth that is dumb, lifeless, and without expression. Whatever secret it may contain cannot be conveyed by normal means. In the midst of her act of contrition, a missile strikes the church, and the priest Zerchi is pinned under the debris. As he lies there, waiting to die, Mrs. Grales reappears, unhurt but changed. Her vestigial head is now "awake" though still capable of repeating only whatever words are addressed to it. Zerchi notices also that the woman seems younger, and that her old "head" is gradually withering away. Something new has awakened in her. What happens next is extraordinary. Fearing that she may have suffered fatal exposure to radiation, Zerchi attempts to bless her. He is repulsed and suffers a temporary blackout from the pain of his wounds. When he awakens, he sees Mrs. Grales kneeling before him:

> *Finally he could make out that she was holding the golden cup in her left hand and in her right, delicately between thumb and forefinger, a single Host. She was offering it to him ... she made no conventional gestures, but the reverence with which she ... handled it convinced him of one thing: she sensed the presence under the veil.*[99]

Thus, in the moment between death and life, with a new holocaust about to commence, a miracle occurs: the dead half of mankind awakens or is healed and dispenses a blessing upon the hurts of creation. The part that had been dead to the mysteries sees beyond the veils of matter into the heart of things. The symbolism of the Eucharist and the Mass performed with the Grail is overt. Mrs. Grales even has five wounds, one of which is described as caused by "a spear of glass," like the wounds inflicted on Christ with the Grail lance. With almost his last breath, the priest murmurs the words of the Catholic hymn *Magnificat*, wanting:

> *to teach her the words as his last act, for he was certain that she shared something with the Maiden who first had spoken them ... he did not ask why God would choose to raise up a creature of primal innocence from the shoulder*

of Mrs Grales or why God should give to it the preternatural gifts of Eden …
[But] he had seen innocence in those eyes and a promise of resurrection.[99]

That "promise of resurrection" has always been inherent in the Grail stories; it is one of the reasons we still seek it. Nor should it be necessary to wait for a distant future to discover it. The paradox may well be that in writing or reading of that future we somehow create it, bringing back from the country outside time the knowledge we require.

Science fiction writers are constantly seeking a paradigm of hope for the future and have frequently turned to the mythos of Arthur for this. What makes their use of the Grail story so apposite is that this was precisely the use of the earliest sacred vessels. The mystery and meaning of the Grail has not changed at all in the thousands of years and dozens of shapes through which it has passed.

One other novel deserves mention here for the way it casts new light on the ancient story of the Grail. *Corbenic* by Catherine Fisher uses the simple device of placing the basic Perceval story into a contemporary setting. It follows Cal, a disaffected teenager with an alcoholic, voice-haunted mother, who sets out to better himself in the world and finds himself caught up in an age-old mythic quest for healing. This could easily have been a clumsy, blatant adaptation, but instead it is both subtle and profound. Cal encounters a medieval reenactment group calling themselves the Company, who may be Arthur and his men, but the truth is left nicely enigmatic. Fisher's knowledge of the Arthurian cycle – especially the Welsh stories – is considerable and her weaving of character and reference into the fabric of the story is deft and never holds up the action. She shows how the Grail can function in the present world and how important it is to connect with the myths that underpin human society.

THE DA VINCI CODE

Another novel that has recently made the Grail something of a *cause célèbre* is *The Da Vinci Code*. Dan Brown's phenomenal bestseller has been taken up by a new generation of seekers and trumpeted as a valuable document tracing the true nature of the Grail and the awesome secret it hides. In fact, the book simply assembles a patchwork of disconnected fragments of knowledge into what is, on the surface at least, a believable scenario.

The book's hero, Harvard professor Robert Langdon, who specializes in the subject of symbology, has previously had strange and semioccult encounters in an earlier book. Now Langdon is plunged headlong into a new adventure when a curator of the Louvre is murdered, leaving a cryptic message scrawled in his own blood. Langdon, teaming up with gifted cryptographer Sophie Neveu, soon finds himself caught up in a web of intrigue involving the Vatican, the Catholic organization known as Opus Dei, and a secret society called the Priory of Sion, which has guarded an ancient secret for centuries. The secret, when it is finally revealed after a series of chases, murders, and assignations, proves to be no less than the existence of a family descended from Jesus, who, having escaped the Crucifixion, married Mary Magdalene and founded a lineage of kings whose descendants may still be alive today.

The Da Vinci Code *suggests that clues to the Grail lie beneath the pyramid of the Louvre museum in Paris.*

Such is the essence of this sensationalist book, which as a straightforward thriller makes for a good afternoon's reading. However, the author has gone to some lengths to research the ideas found in the book, in particular the fact that the Church has attempted to hide and subvert the truth about Jesus and the Magdalene and of the existence of a hidden feminine influence in the development of Christianity. This has sparked a controversy, which, in turn, has spawned something of an industry of books seeking either to break the so-called code hidden in the paintings of Leonardo da Vinci or to debunk the whole book on the grounds that it is really an attack on the Church. That so much attention should be directed toward this fictional account would be extraordinary were it not for the fact that at the heart of the theory is just enough truth to capture the imagination and feed a growing need for humanity to find the true meaning at the heart of religion and our own place within it.

Yet there is nothing new in the book at all. Most of what it discusses is traceable to one or another of the chapters of the Grail's long history. All have been discussed here, or have been written about already. Another book, equally sensational in its representation of the facts of the Grail, but at least presented as factual, appeared over twenty years ago and caused an even greater stir. This was *The Holy Blood and the*

Holy Grail by Michael Baigent, Henry Lincoln, and Richard Leigh. Their book started a veritable avalanche of follow-up volumes, each one aimed at expanding the original idea. The old pattern of Grail quest material, germinating from a single seed and giving birth to numerous more complex offshoots, is again seen to be in operation, although in a very different way.

THE HOLY BLOOD

Baigent, Lincoln, and Leigh became overnight celebrities when their book appeared, and for months afterward the Grail was on everyone's lips. The book set out to investigate an ancient mystery – that of the sacred bloodlines of European royalty – and to connect it with the Grail by way of the scribal error mentioned in an earlier chapter, which changed San Greal (Holy Grail) to Sang Real (Royal Blood). From this, by dint of a complex web of evidence, which connected the Cathars, the Templars, and an ancient French dynasty, the authors set out to prove that the Grail really referred to the bloodline of Christ, who, as in Dan Brown's book, escapes death on the Cross, marries Mary Magdalene, and founds the ill-fated Merovingian line. Much of this was presented in fictionalized form in Liz Green's novel *The Dreamer of the Vine.*

German researcher Walter Johannes Stein thought the Grail could be hidden somewhere in the French Pyrenees.

Much of this ground had been covered in an earlier work by German Grail expert Walter Johannes Stein, but Baigent, Lincoln, and Leigh took it a step further and brought the story up to date with the inclusion of the mysterious sect known as the Priory of Sion. This group, for which virtually no documentary evidence exists any earlier than the 1930s, claims descent from both the Merovingian kings of France and the Knights Templar, and numbers among its members Leonardo, Botticelli, Isaac Newton, and Victor Hugo. They are also, according to Baigent, Lincoln, and Leigh, the inheritors of the Holy Blood – that of Christ, whom they portray as a king and a charismatic leader, rather than the Messiah or Son of God.

In this scenario, the Grail is seen as a bloodline rather than an actual object, and the archetypal participants in the quest are replaced by actual figures who played leading roles in the

history of the world. We are left with a political jigsaw crossed with a treasure hunt. The priest Berenger Saunière (after whom the murdered curator at the beginning of Brown's book is named), seems to have discovered either documents or actual treasure while renovating his church at Rennes-le-Château in 1891. He has become the subject of numerous books and studies seeking to relate his finds to the secret history of the European bloodlines.

There is, however, little or no real evidence to support the claims made in the book. Far too many of those who offered information to the authors' theory either vanished mysteriously or were not contactable. Much of the book seems little more than a clever manipulation of historical facts with the addition of unprovable speculations. These detract from a serious understanding of the Grail tradition, and to trivialize it into physical treasure-trove rather than helping to penetrate its true mystery. Recent explorations by Laurence Gardiner in his books *Bloodline of the Holy Grail* and *Genesis of the Grail Kings* have carried this even further, establishing a chain of possible evidence for a family of Grail guardians stretching back before the actual period of the Grail romances and forward into the present time. However, his evidence for this rests solely on genealogical documents that have as yet to be produced by way of evidence.

THE SPEAR OF DESTINY

The relic known as the lance of Longinus is believed to be that which pierced the side of Christ.

Baigent, Lincoln, and Leigh fail to even mention Walter Stein, whose book *World History in the Light of the Grail* also traced the major characters of the Grail cycle to the Merovingian and Carolingian dynasties, though his researches parallel their own. Unfortunately, Stein's one-time association with the Nazis has cast his work under a shadow even though he left Germany soon after the start of World War II and came to work for Winston Churchill as an "occult adviser." Stein's theories, which also relate to the whereabouts of the so-called lance of Longinus, were elaborated by Trevor Ravenscroft in his book *The Spear of Destiny*. Here it is suggested that the power of the Grail can be sought with equal determination by those who seek to misuse its power. The German dictator Adolf Hitler, who believed implicitly in the value of occult attack as a reinforcement of physical war, sent teams of researchers in quest of the Hallows of the Grail and spear. The ruins of the Cathar citadel at Montségur, which was the setting for the darkest days in the Albigensian Crusade, were excavated in expectation of discovering one or another. The spear, fragments of which had been traced to Rome and the Austro-Hungarian Empire, did find their way into Nazi hands for a time, and the infamous leader of the Schutzstaffel (SS), Heinrich Himmler, formed an elite core of officers around it at a castle aptly named Black Camelot.

Part of the spear now resides in the Vatican, though it is not known whether it is the true original, or like many of the Grail relics scattered throughout the world, simply a forgery that has become invested with power through the belief of those who accepted it as real.

THE MAGDALENIAN GRAIL

The association of the Magdalene with the Grail in these books and others has led to some interesting speculations, primarily that this elusive figure assumed a far more significant importance in the Middle Ages as a representative of woman as "penitent whore." Much of this idea derives from Gnosticism, which was an ancient form of esoteric Christianity founded upon even older principles. The Magdalene is mentioned in the Gnostic Gospel of Philip as Jesus' constant companion, whom he loves above all the rest of the disciples and frequently kisses upon the mouth. In another Gnostic text we find her still communicating directly with the Messiah some time after the events of the Crucifixion, a fact that enrages the disciple Peter and is an apparent foundation for much of the subsequent fear and hatred of women expressed by the Church fathers. Certainly, Mary's own words as reported in the Gnostic *Pistis Sophia*, suggest this: "Peter makes me hesitate," she says. "I am afraid of him, for he hates the female race."[67]

This unusual medieval painting by Michael Wolgemuth shows three Maries: Mary, the Mother of Jesus, Mary Salome and Mary Magdalene.

It is perhaps not surprising that a connection between such groups as the Cathars and Templars, both of whom are said to have venerated the Magdalene and the stories of the Grail, should have become such an essential part of contemporary speculation about the sacred vessel. There are no specific connections between the two themes that can be traced to a reliable source, but the simple fact of the growth of heretical ideas at the same time as the codification of the Grail story are suggestive enough to make this a popular misconception.

But it is not necessary to import the figure of the Magdalene to provide a feminine aspect within the Grail stories. It is present already in the form of Sophia, the Shekinah, the Virgin Mary, and Dindrane, the sister of Perceval.

MODERN RELICS

The well at Chalice Gardens, Glastonbury, Somerset, is said to have been the hiding place of the Grail.

Following the appearance of such sensational books as *The Holy Blood and the Holy Grail* and *The Da Vinci Code*, there has been an increasingly large outpouring of new theories, each declaring that the Grail has been found at last. Behind these arguments lies a desperate need to understand the true mystery of the Grail. This has resulted in a spate of relic hunting that comes directly from a desire to find an actual Grail. Throughout the Middle Ages, a number of objects were believed to be the actual Grail of Christ. Not surprisingly, in more recent times, Grail-hunters have also sought to find actual physical objects that they believe to be the original sacred vessel.

In the early twentieth century two such objects received a great deal of public attention and continue to exert their own particular fascination today. The first is a small blue bowl, discovered beneath a well head in the Somerset town of Glastonbury and subsequently declared to be the Grail. Historical investigations indicated that the bowl may have originated in the Holy Land and that its dates place it close to the events of Christ's ministry. Other investigators have suggested that it is medieval glass of the kind found and made in the city of Venice. However, such is the strength of belief in the power of the blue bowl that pilgrims still go to be in its presence, many declaring that it possesses an aura of sanctity. Slightly earlier than this, a small wooden cup, kept for many years in a house at Nanteos in Wales, has also had its adherents. Like the Grail of medieval stories, this relic had its guardians, the Powell family. During the 1930s the cup was openly displayed at Nanteos House, and the belief in its curative powers was widely accepted. People came from far and wide in search of healing. Many of those who drank from the cup took to biting small pieces from the rim in order to keep a fragment of the sacred vessel. This resulted in its being withdrawn and kept in a bank vault for safety. It has been tested and carbon-dated, and evidence suggests that it is indeed as old as the first century CE, though others have advanced a medieval origin. Certainly, this simple wooden cup is far more likely to have been used in the ceremony of the first Eucharist; whether it is the actual cup used by Jesus and his disciples remains a matter for the individual.

The Nanteos Cup is one of several vessels considered at one time or another to have been the Grail. Pilgrims in search of its avowed healing properties bit pieces from it, leaving only a shallow fragment of the original cup.

These objects and others like them remain the subject of speculation and curiosity. Behind the almost obsessive seeking for such relics lies a very human desire to touch the infinite. Just as the medieval knights in the Arthurian epics went in search of the Grail in order to encounter God more directly, so modern Grail-seekers, no matter how they perceive deity, have sought to discover the secrets of the Grail for much the same reason. In each case and with each new theory put forward, the Grail seems to retreat further from our understanding. Many arguments as to the appropriateness of such a search could be put forward, one way or another. Almost certainly there will always be those who seek a physical object. However, it is my belief that such research is fruitless and that any such object discovered, no matter how powerful, will only begin to scratch the surface of the true mystery of the Grail. The quest must always be a personal one, whether it is carried out via an exploration of the ideas represented by the Grail, or by visiting sacred sites in the hope of catching a glimpse of the sacred vessel.

THE TRUE GRAIL

One of the reasons for the present book is to show that it is not necessary to buy into any of these theories, fascinating though they may be, to see into the heart of the Grail. Of course, the Church has its secrets; how could such an ancient and intricate organization fail to do so? But when all is said and done, does it really make any difference whether Jesus and Mary Magdalene had children? It might have mattered to the medieval dynasty that claimed this descent – but now? Such matters are best relegated to the category of fascinating speculations. They most certainly do not contribute to any understanding of the true secrets of the Grail.

This portrait of Mary Magdalene from the fifteenth-century Sforza Book of Hours, *shows her as a holy figure carried to heaven by angels.*

Just what these secrets are is ultimately a matter for each individual following their own personal quest. For me, the Grail remains an idea that represents a most vital aspect of human life, the ability to commune with a spiritual source, no matter what we may mean by the word. As such, it is far more powerful than any physical representation that might be discovered anywhere and at any moment, whether on the altar of a church, in a mountain cave in the Middle East, or in some distant utopian world.

Myths tell us who we are and who we were. They are memories of things and events that were once more important to us, when our species was first emerging from the primal swamp. The Grail is just one such a myth. It reminds us of a lost state of innocence, a paradisal state we gave up for the sake of knowledge. But it is also a way back to our ancient home, a passageway that constantly opens up before us. This opportunity to return makes the Grail so important that it has continued to resonate within us up to the present moment, when we still seek the same goals as our ancestors and still turn to the idea of the Grail to help us understand our journey.

The Grail has been a constant companion on that journey through the ages, offering a way to reach out toward the infinite from the days when our first ancestors began to shape clay vessels that were elegant and imbued with magical potency. Throughout antiquity, the kraters, cauldrons, and cups that kept alive the mystery at the heart of the Grail continued to be acknowledged as doorways to the infinite. The message they brought was nothing new and never varied in all of this time. Only the means of achieving the mystery changed. Aspects of the Grail appear and disappear, reflecting the needs of each succeeding age. In our own time it represents both the need to revise our place in the universe and of our relationship with deity. As such, it will doubtless continue to offer us a road to self-fulfillment, a means of journeying outside the sphere of our self-imposed limitations.

The subject of the Grail is an intensely personal thing. Whether we choose to see it as an idea or an impulse or as a physical object is, in the end, irrelevant. What does matter is that we should continue to search for the wonder it represents.

At the end of the great medieval narrative *Perlesvaus*, when the Arthurian quest for the Grail is long over, the castle where the sacred vessel was once kept still stands, empty now, but still haunted by the ghostly presence of the events that took place there. The book is set in a mythical past, as are all of the Arthurian stories of the time, but it is in historic time that three young knights set out to visit the place, to discover for themselves the truth of the rumors they had grown up with. The anonymous author of the work tells us what happened:

> *Full of excitement they entered the castle. They remained there for a long time, and when they emerged they lived as hermits, wandering the paths of the forest, eating only roots. When people asked why they lived thus, they would only say: "Go where we went and you will see why."*[13]

The same is true for all who continue to seek the Grail, in whatever form or by whatever means. We are all on the quest – and we will all discover something of what it has to offer. This is the truth of the Grail.

REFERENCES AND FURTHER READING

1. Adolf, H. *Visio Pacis: Holy City and Grail.* Philadelphia, Pennsylvania State University Press, 1960
2. Allen, P. M. (ed.). *A Christian Rosenkreutz Anthology.* New York, Rudolf Steiner Publications, 1981
3. Anderson, P. *A Midsummer Tempest.* New York, Del Rey, 1978
4. Annet, S. F. *Grail Lectures.* New Jersey, CI, Servants of the Light, 1986
5. Baigent, M., R. Leigh and H. Lincoln. *The Holy Blood and the Holy Grail.* London, Jonathan Cape, 1982
6. Barron, W. R. J. (ed.). *The Voyage of St. Brendan.* Exeter, University of Exeter Press, 2002
7. Bartrum, P. C. "The Thirteen Treasures of the Island of Britain," *Etudes celtiques,* Vol. 10, pp. 435–77, 1963
8. Bernard of Clairvaux. *On the Song of Songs.* Michigan, Cistercian Publications, 1976
9. Bernard of Clairvaux. *Treatise in Praise of the New Knighthood.* Michigan, Cistercian Publications, 1977
10. Bothwell-Gosse, A. *The Rose Immortal.* London, Watkins, 1958
11. Brock, K. S. *St. Ephraem: The Harp of the Spirit.* London, Fellowship of St. Alban and St. Sergius, 1975
12. Brown, D. *The Da Vinci Code.* New York and London, Doubleday, 2003
13. Bryant, N. *The High Book of the Grail.* Cambridge, D. S. Brewer, 1978
14. Bryant, N. *Merlin and the Grail: Joseph of Arimathea, Merlin, Perceval: A Trilogy of Arthurian Romances Attributed to Robert de Borron.* Cambridge, D. S. Brewer, 2001
15. Bryant, N. *The Legend of the Grail.* Cambridge, D. S. Brewer, 2004
16. Campbell, J. *The Hero with a Thousand Faces.* Princeton, N.J., Princeton University Press, 1949
17. Campbell, J. *Masks of Gods.* London, Souvenir Press 1968–9
18. Campbell, J. *Myths to Live By.* London, Souvenir Press, 1973
19. Campbell, J. *The Inner Reaches of Outer Space.* New York, Alfred van der Marck Editions, 1985
20. Campbell, J. *The Power of Myth.* New York, Bantam Doubleday, 1988
21. Campbell, D. E. (trans.). *The Tale of Balain.* Evanston, Northwestern University Press, 1972

22. Capellanus, Andreas (trans. J. J. Parry). *The Art of Courtly Love*. New York, W. W. Norton, 1941

23. Cavendish, R. *King Arthur and the Grail*. London, Weidenfeld & Nicolson, 1978

24. Chrétien de Troyes. (trans. D. D. R. Owen). *Arthurian Romances*. London, J. M. Dent, 1987

25. Cooper-Oakley, I. *Masonry and Medieval Mysticism*. London, Theosophical Publishing House, 1977

26. Cox, Simon. *Cracking the Da Vinci Code*. London, Michael O'Mara, 2004

27. Cross, T. P. and C. H. Slover. *Ancient Irish Tales*. Dublin, Figgis, 1936

28. Currer-Briggs, N. *The Shroud and the Grail*. London, Weidenfeld & Nicolson, 1987

29. Day, M. L. (ed. and trans.). *The Story of Meriadoc, King of Cumbria*. New York, Garland, 1988

30. Delaforge, G. *The Templar Tradition in the Age of Aquarius*. Vermont, Threshold Books, 1987

31. Denning, M. and O. Phillips. *Magical Philosophy* (5 vols.). Minnesota, Llewellyn Press, 1974–9

32. De Sede, G. *Les Templiers*. Paris, J'ai Lu, 1969

33. De Sede, G. *La Rose Croix*. Paris, J'ai Lu, 1978

34. De Rougemont, D. *Passion and Society*. London, Faber & Faber, 1955

35. Evans, S. *In Quest of the Holy Grail*. London, J. M. Dent, 1898

36. Firdausi, *The Shah Nameh*. (ed. A. G. Warner and E. Warner). London, Routledge, 2000

37. Fisher, Catherine. *Corbenic*. London, Red Fox, 2002

38. Gadal, A. *Sur le chemin de San Grail*, Harlaam, Rosencruis-Pers, 1979

39. Gantz, J. (trans.). *The Mabinogion*. Harmondsworth, Penguin Books, 1985

40. Gardner, E. *Arthurian Legends in Italian Literature*. New York, Octagon Books, 1971

41. Gardner, L. *Bloodline of the Holy Grail*. Shaftesbury, Element Books, 1996

42. Gardner, L. *Genesis of the Grail Kings*. London and New York, Bantam, 2000

43. Geoffrey of Monmouth. (trans. J. J. Parry). *The Vita Merlini*. Urbana, University of Illinois Press, 1925

44. Geoffrey of Monmouth. (trans. Lewis Thorpe). *The History of the Kings of Britain*. Harmondsworth, Penguin Books, 1966

45. Gerald of Wales. *The Journey Through Wales*. Harmonsworth, Penguin Books, 1978

46. *The Golden Blade*, Issue No. 33. Rudolf Steiner Press, 1981

47. Gray, W. G. *The San Grail Sacrament*. Maine, Weiser, 1986

48. Green, Liz. *The Dreamer on the Vine*. Bodley Head, 1980.

49. Griffin, J. B. *The Holy Grail: The Legend, the History, the Evidence*. Jefferson, NC, Mcfarland & Co., 2001

50. Grossinger, R. (ed.). *The Alchemical Tradition*. California, North Atlantic Books, 1983

51. Gryffydd, W. J. *Math Vab Mathonwy*. Cardiff, University of Wales Press, 1928

52. Gryffydd, W. J. *Rhiannon*. Cardiff University of Wales Press, 1953

53. Guest, Lady C. *The Mabinogion*. Cardiff, John Jones, 1977

54. Hall, M. P. *Orders of the Quest: The Holy Grail*. Los Angeles, Philosophical Research Society, 1976

55. Heinrich von dem Tulin (trans. D. W. Thomas). *The Crown (Diu Crone)*. Nebraska, University of Nebraska Press, 1989

56. Jacobus de Voraginie. *The Golden Legend*. London, Penguin Books, 1999

57. James, M. R. ed. *The Apocryphal New Testament*. Oxford, Oxford University Press, 1924

58. Jung, C. G. and M. L. von Franz. *The Grail Legends*. London, Hodder & Stoughton, 1971

59. Jung, C. G. *Memories, Dreams and Reflections*. London, Routledge, 1989

60. Kahane, H. and R. *The Krater and the Grail: Hermetic Sources of the Parzival*. Urbana, University of Illinois Press, 1954

61. Kirby, W. F. trans. *Kalevala: The Land of Heroes*. London and New York, Dutton, 1907

62. Knappert, J. *The Encyclopaedia of Middle Eastern Mythology and Religion*. Shaftsbury, Dorset, Element Books, 1993

63. Knight, G. *The Secret Tradition in Arthurian Legend*. Boston, Weiser Books, 1996

64. Lacy, N. J. (ed.). *The Old French Arthurian Vulgate and Post Vulgate in Translation* (5 vols.). New York, Garland Publishing, 1993–9

65. Lacy, N. J. and G. Ashe. *The Arthurian Handbook*. New York, Garland Publishing, 1986

66. Lambert, M. D. *Medieval Heresy*. Arnold, 1977

67. Lecarrier, J. *The Gnostics*. London, Peter Owen, 1973

68. Levy, G. R. *The Sword from the Rock*. London, Faber & Faber, 1953

69. Lewis, C. B. *Classical Mythology and Arthurian Romance*. Oxford, Oxford University Press, 1932

70. Lievegoed, B. C. J. *Mystery Streams in Europe and the New Mysteries*. New York, Anthroposophic Press, 1982

71. Lindsay, J. *The Troubadours and their World*. London, Frederick Muller, 1982

72. Littleton, C. S. and L. A. Melcor. *From Scythia to Camelot*. London and New York, Garland Publishing, 2000

73. Loomis, R. S. *Celtic Myth and Arthurian Romance*. New York, Columbia University Press, 1927

74. Loomis, R. S. *Wales and the Arthurian Legend*. Cardiff, University of Wales Press, 1956

75. Loomis, R. S. *The Development of Arthurian Romance*. New York, Norton, 1963

76. Macalister, R. S. *Lebor Gabala Erenn*. Dublin, Institute for Advanced Studies, 1941

77. Macgregor, R. *Indiana Jones and the Last Crusade*. London, Sphere Books, 1989

78. Magre, M. *The Return of the Magi*. London, Sphere Books, 1957

79. Malory, Sir Thomas, (ed. J. Matthews). *Le Morte D'Arthur* London, Cassell & Co., 2000

80. Marie de France. *Lais* (trans. G. S. Burgess and & K. Busby). Harmondsworth, Penguin Books, 1986

81. Markale, J. *King Arthur King of Kings*. London, Gordon Cremonesi, 1977

82. Matarasso, P. *The Quest of the Grail*. Harmondsworth, Penguin Books, 1969

83. Matthews, C. *Elements of Celtic Tradition*. Shaftesbury, Dorset, Element Books, 1989

84. Matthews, C. *King Arthur and the Goddess of the Land*. Rochester, VT, Inner Traditions, 2002

85. Matthews, C. *Mabon and the Heroes of Celtic Britain*. Rochester, VT, Inner Traditions, 2002

86. Matthews, C. *Sophia: Goddess of Wisdom, Bride of God*. Wheaton, IL, Quest Books, 2003

87. Matthews, C. and J. *Hallowquest: Tarot Magic and the Arthurian Mysteries*. London, HarperCollins, 1990

88. Matthews, C. and J. *Ladies of the Lake*. London, HarperCollins, 1992

89. Matthews, C. and J. *Walkers Between the Worlds*. Rochester, VT, Inner Traditions, 2003

90. Matthews, J. *The Grail: Quest for Eternal Life*. London, Thames & Hudson, 1981

91. Matthews, J. *An Arthurian Reader*. London, HarperCollins, 1988

92. Matthews, J. *Healing the Wounded King*. Shaftesbury, Dorset, Element Books, 1997

93. Matthews, J. *Sources of the Grail*. Edinburgh, Floris Books, 1997

94. Matthews, J. *At the Table of the Grail*. London, Watkins Books, 2000

95. Matthews, J. *Gawain, Knight of the Goddess*. Inner Traditions, 2001

96. Matthews, J. *Taliesin: the Last Celtic Shaman*. Rochester, VT, Inner Traditions, 2001

97. Matthews, J. and M. Green. *The Grail Seekers Companion* (revised ed.) Thoth Books, 2003

98. Matthews, J. and R. J. Stewart. *Warriors of Arthur*. Poole, Dorset, Blandford Press, 1987

99. Miller, W. M. *A Canticle for Leibowitz*. Philadelphia, Lippincott, 1960

100. Moorcock, M. *The War Hound of the World's Pain*. London, New English Library, 1982

101. Morgan, G. (ed.). *Nanteos*. Llandysul, Ceredigan, Gomer, 2001

102. Newstead, H. *Bran the Blessed in Arthurian Romance*. New York, Columbia University Press, 1939

103. Oldenbourg, Z. *Massacre at Montsegur*. London, Weidenfeld & Nicholson, 1961

104. Panikkar, R. *The Vedic Experience*. Mamtramanjan Delhi, Motilal Banarsidass Publishers, 1977

105. Plato. (ed. Edith Hamilton and Huntington Cairns). *The Complete Dialogues*. Princeton, NJ, Princeton University Press, 1961

105a. Plotinus *The Enneads*. (trans Stephen MacKenna), London, Medici Press, 1917–32

106. Plutarch. (trans. F. C. Babbitt). *Moralia*. London, Heinemann, 1957

107. Quispel, G. *Tatian and the Gospel of Thomas*. Leiden, E. J. Brill, 1975

108. Ralls, Karen. *The Templars and the Grail*. Wheaton, IL, Quest Books, 2003

109. Ravenscroft, T. *The Cup of Destiny*. London, Rider, 1981

110. Ravenscroft, T. *Spear of Destiny*. London, Neville Spearman 1972

111. Robinson, J. M. (ed.). *Nag Hammadi Library*. Leiden, E. J. Brill, 1977

112. Rolt-Wheeler, F. *Mystic Gleams from the Holy Grail*. London, Rider Books, 1945

113. Runciman, S. *The Medieval Manichee*. Cambridge, Cambridge University Press, 1969

114. Schlauch, M. *Medieval Narrative*. New York, Gordian Press, 1969

115. Skeate, W. W. *Joseph of Arimathea*. London, Early English Texts Society, 1871

116. Skeeles, D. *The Romance of Perceval in Prose*. Seattle, University of Washington Press, 1966

117. Slessarev, V. *Prester John: The Letter*. Minneapolis, University of Minnesota Press, 1959

118. Stein, W. J. *The Ninth Century and the Holy Grail Temple*. London, Lodge Press, 1989

119. Steiner, R. *Christ and the Spiritual World, and the Search for the Holy Grail*. London, Rudolph Steiner Press, 1963

120. Steiner, R. *Occult Science: An Outline*. London, Rudolf Steiner Press, 1979

121. Stewart, R. J. *The Prophetic Vision of Merlin*. Arkana, 1986

122. Stewart, R. J. *The Mystic Life of Merlin*. Arkana, 1986

122a. Traherne, T. *Poetical Works*, London, Faith Press, 1963

123. von Scharfenburg, A. (ed. W. Wolf). *Der Jungere Titurel*. Berlin, publisher unknown, 1955 and 1968

124. Waite, A. E. *The Hidden Church of the Holy Grail*. London, Redman, 1909

125. Waite, A. E. *The Holy Grail: Its Legends and Symbolism*. Rider, 1933

126. Wallace-Murphy, T. and M. Hopkins. *Rosslyn*. Shaftesbury, Dorset, Element Books, 1999

127. Weston, J. L. *From Ritual to Romance*. New York, Doubleday, 1957

128. Williams, C. *The Descent of the Dove*. London, Faber & Faber, 1939

129. Williams, C. *War in Heaven*. London, Faber & Faber, 1952

130. Williams, C. *Taliesin Through Logres and The Region of the Summer Stars*. Cambridge, D. S. Brewer, 1982

131. Williams, C. and C. S. Lewis. *Arthurian Torso*. Oxford, Oxford University Press, 1948

132. Wilson, P. L. *Ploughing the Clouds: The Search for Irish Soma*. San Francisco, City Lights, 1999

133. Wolfram von Eschenbach. (trans. A. Hatto). *Parzival*. Harmondsworth, Penguin Books, 1980

134. Zelazny, R. *Last Defender of Camelot*. London, Sphere Books, 1986

INDEX

ACKNOWLEDGMENTS

Unless otherwise stated, all translations
are by the author.

Allen, Paul M. (ed.). "Castle Karlstein,"
  "Fludd," and "Thomas Vaughan" in
  A Christian Rosenkreutz Anthology.
  New York, Rudolf Steiner
  Publications, 1981
Bernard of Clairvaux. *Treatise in Praise
  of the New Knighthood*. Michigan,
  Cistercian Publishers, 1977
Bothwell-Gosse, A. *The Rose Immortal*.
  London, Watkins, 1958
Bryant, Nigel. (trans.). *Perlesvaus.
  The High Book of the Holy Grail*.
  Cambridge, Boydell & Brewer,
  1978
Campbell, Joseph. *Hero With A
  Thousand Faces*. Princeton University
  Press, 1949
Campbell, Joseph. *Myths to Live By*.
  London, Souvenir Press, 1973
Cross, T. P. and C. H. Slover. "Baile in
  Scail" in *Ancient Irish Tales*. Dublin,
  Figgis, 1936
Evans, Sebastian (trans.). *The
  Elucidation* in *In Quest of the Holy
  Grail*. London, J. M. Dent, 1898
Flamel, Nicholas. [source unknown]

Gardner, E. Jacobus de Voraigne quoted
  in *Arthurian Legends in Italian
  Literature*. New York, Octagon
  Books, 1971
James, M. R. Acts of Thomas in *The
  Apocryphal New Testament*. Oxford,
  Oxford University Press
Joseph of Arimathea. EETS, London,
  1888
Jung, C. G. *Memories, Dreams and
  Reflections*. (ed. A. Jaffe). London,
  Routledge, 1989
Kirby, W. F. (trans.). *Kalevala*. London,
  J. M. Dent, 1907
Magre, Maurice. Templar confession
  and "Templars Pardon" in *The Return
  of the Magi*. Sphere Books, 1957
Malory, Sir Thomas. (ed. John
  Matthews). *Le Morte D'Arthur*.
  London, Cassell & Co., 2000
Matthews, John. "Litany of Loretto" in
  The Grail: Quest for the Eternal.
  London, Thames & Hudson, 1981
Miller, Walter M. *A Canticle for
  Leibowitz*. Philadelphia, Lippincott,
  1960
Moorcock, Michael. *The Warhound of
  the World's Pain*. London, New
  English Library, 1982

Panikkar, Raimundo . *The Vedic Experience*. Mamtramanjan Delhi, Motilal Banarsidass Publishers, 1977

Plato (trans. Benjamin Jowett, ed. E. Hamilton and H. Cairns). *Timaeus. Complete Dialogues*. Princeton, N.J., Princeton University Press, 1961

Plotinus. *Enneads*.

Plutarch (trans. F.C. Babbitt). *Moralia*. London, Heinemann, 1957

Pope, A. U. "Persia and the Holy Grail" in *Sources of the Grail*. (ed. John Matthews). Edinburgh, Floris Books, 1997

Quispel, Giles (trans.). *Gospel of Thomas*. (source unknown)

Slessarev, V. (trans.). *Prester John. The Letter*. Minneapolis, University of Minnesota Press, 1959

St Ephram. *The Harp of the Spirit*. (trans. S. Brock). London, Fellowship of St Alban and St Sergius, 1975

Taylor, Rachel Annand. *Perceval at Corbenic*. (source unknown, 1930s)

Traherne, Thomas, *Poetical Works*, London, Faith Press, 1963

von Eschenbach, Wolfram. *Parzival* (trans A. Hatto). Harmondsworth, Penguin Books, 1980

von Eschenbach, Wolfram. *Parzival: A hero*, 1980

Waite, A. E. *The Holy Grail*. London, 1888

Williams, Charles. *The Descent of the Dove*. London, Faber & Faber, 1939

Williams, Charles . *War in Heaven*. London, Faber & Faber, 1952

PHOTO ACKNOWLEDGMENTS

AKG, London 24, 25, 39, 55, 63, 84, 89, 93, 102, 108, 124, 133, 160; /Erich Lessing 135; /Jean-Louis Nou 116; /Pirozzi 62; /Domingie Rabatti 117; /Visoars 128. **Alamy**/The Photolibrary Wales 41. **Alan Lee** 29. **Ancient Art and Architecture Collection** 1, 23, 47, 126, 129. **British Film Institute Stills, Posters & Designs** 147. **Bibliotheque Royale de Belgique** 99. **Banque d' images** 15, 50, 56, 100. **Bridgeman Art Library, London (www.bridgeman.co.uk)** 7, 77, 91; /Archives Larousse, Paris 144; /Ashmolean Museum, University of Oxford 17; /Bibliotheque Municipale, Cambrai, France 95; /Bibliotheque Nationale, Paris 2, 10, 54, 85, 137; /British Library, London 75, 110, 122; /Centre Historique des Archives Nationale, Paris 115; /Christie's, London 157; /Sally Elliot 18; /Louvre, Paris, France 109, 142, 154;

/Paul Maeyaert 53; /Musee des Antiquities Nationales, France 21, 31; /Museo de Santa Cruz, Toledo, Spain 119; /Private Collection, Boltin Picture Library 27; /Private Collection, Roger-Viollet, Paris 145; /San Francesco, Arezzo, Italy 49; /Sir Geoffrey Keynes Collection, Cambridgeshire 9; /Torre Abbey, Devon 36; /Walker Art Gallery, Liverpool 66. **British Library** 65. **Christie's Images, London** 22. **Collections** 45. **Corbis UK Ltd**/Bettmann 146; /Burnstein Collection 103; /Greenhalf Photography 158; /Tim Hawkins 59; /E. O. Hoppe 141; /Earl and Nazima Kowall 98; /Chris Lisle 112; /Francis G. Mayer 13; /Homer Sykes 151; /Adam Woolfitt 35. **Fortean Picture Library** 156. **Garden World Images** 19. **John Matthews** 121. **Mary Evans Picture Library** 78. **Miranda Gray** 42. **The Picture Desk Limited**/Art archive 71, 97, 107; Kobal Collection 148. **Royal Commission on the Ancient and Historical Monuments of Wales**/Crown 159. **Science Photo Library** 82. **Tate Gallery Publications, London** 68. **Temple Lodge Publishing** 155. **TopFoto** 138.

To find out more about John Matthews, visit his web site at *Hallowquest.org.uk*